Deciphering a Civil Code

Deciphering a Civil Code

Sources of Law and Methods of Interpretation

Alain A. Levasseur

HERMANN MOYSE, SR. AND HENRY PLAUCHÉ DART PROFESSOR OF LAW
FONDATION POUR LE DROIT CONTINENTAL
2014–2016 LOUISIANA BAR FOUNDATION SCHOLAR-IN-RESIDENCE
LOUISIANA STATE UNIVERSITY LAW CENTER

Foreword
James L. Dennis
CIRCUIT JUDGE, UNITED STATES COURT OF APPEALS
FIFTH CIRCUIT

With the support of
The Louisiana Bar Foundation

With the assistance of
Kimberly Ulasiewicz, Beth Williams, Susan Gualtier

CAROLINA ACADEMIC PRESS
Durham, North Carolina

Library of Congress Cataloging-in-Publication Data

Levasseur, Alain A., author.
  Deciphering a civil code : sources of laws and methods of interpretation /
Alain A. Levasseur.
      pages cm
  Includes bibliographical references and index.
  ISBN 978-1-61163-634-5 (alk. paper)
  1. Civil law--Codification. 2. Civil law--Interpretation and construction. 3.
Law--Codification. I. Title.

K623.L495 2015
340.5'6--dc23

                    2015013324

Carolina Academic Press
700 Kent Street
Durham, North Carolina 27701
Telephone (919) 489-7486
Fax (919) 493-5668
www.cap-press.com

Printed in Canada

This book is dedicated, first and foremost, to my wife, Susan, whose love and many encouragements made this book a "dream" come true. Many sincere thanks to my children and grandchildren for the depth of their feelings and loving strength of the family they have built around my wife and me.

Contents

Part II · Interpretation and Reasoning

Foreword

As Professor Levasseur explains in *Deciphering a Civil Code*, a civil code is more than just a systematic collection of private law rules, standards and precepts that precisely commands the resolution of legal issues foreseen by the codifiers. It is also a living, breathing organism of succinctly integrated civil law principles capable of addressing novel future questions that the codifiers themselves could not have anticipated. To properly interpret and apply a civil code requires understanding how its three sources of doctrine, jurisprudence, and legislation have combined in its codification; and how the expositors of the three—the courts, the scholars, and the legislators—must continue to cooperate for the code's successful implementation.

Professor Levasseur's purpose in this concise and pithy work is to dispel some misunderstandings of what a civil code is and how it may be used in the work of lawyers, judges and legislators. He describes the evolutionary development of the French Civil Code of 1804 and the Louisiana Civil Codes of 1808 and 1825 from their roots in Roman and Canonical law through the pre-revolutionary laws of France. Along the way, we are given insights into the thinking of many who birthed and shaped the civil law tradition that ultimately resulted in the codifications, such as Gaius, Justinian, Bartolus, Domat, Pothier, Portalis, and Napoléon, as well as the immensely important post-codification scholar Gény. Included, also, are tips on how the civil code is designed to govern not as "a pure act of power" but as "an act of wisdom, justice and reason," as Portalis put it, and "that in drafting a civil code, a few precise provisions on each subject would suffice and that the great art is to simplify everything while foreseeing everything." There is a significant passage as to how the language of a civil code is best derived from that of ordinary citizens but elevated to general principles in an elegantly economical style. To provide mental discipline in applying the code, Professor Levasseur describes and illustrates methods of reasoning developed in the use of the codes. Finally, as an overall exegesis, he brings to bear all of the foregoing in a line-by-line analysis and critique of three Louisiana Supreme Court decisions applying the Louisiana Civil Code.

At once concise and exhaustive, this book creates a rare resource for anyone hoping to sharpen her or his skills in the art of interpreting, applying or revising a civil code.

James L. Dennis
Circuit Judge, United States Court of Appeals for the Fifth Circuit

Acknowledgments

This book has been planned, shaped and "carved" out of many years of teaching civil code courses and, in particular, a course on Legal Traditions, a unique offering of the Louisiana State University Law Center. I am therefore indebted to the many generations of students who have inspired me and helped me (some "unwillingly and reluctantly"!) to put this book together.

I am much indebted to the Louisiana Bar Foundation for its support and encouragement in selecting me as its "2014–2016 Scholar-in-Residence," thereby making possible the writing of this book.

I have also greatly benefited, here and in many other instances, from the advice and help of my assistant Kimberly Ulasiewicz and from the support of Beth Williams, Professor and Director of the LSU Law Library. Many thanks to an overburdened but always eager staff of the Law Library, Susan Gualtier among others, for never questioning my many requests for books and articles.

Deciphering a Civil Code

Introduction

The main purpose of this book is to present as clear and as simple as possible an understanding of the cultural, historical and sociological background in the making of a "civil code." We hope that one will then be able to make use of the methods and tools of reasoning that are available to grasp the deeper inner meaning of the contents of a civil code.

Our goal will be best served if we go back in time to the historical roots of the civil law tradition in order to better understand the contemporary meaning of this well recognized combination of the two words "civil" and "code." These two words are identified, in general, with civil law systems, such as the French civil law system illustrated by the French Civil Code that dates back to 1804, and also, to some extent, with mixed legal systems that have a "civil code" as is the case of the mixed legal system of the State of Louisiana since 1808 and 1825. For historical and cultural reasons, which are also natural and logical reasons, these two civil codes will be our essential grounds of inquiry and analysis.[1]

1. The Meaning of "Civil" in the Expression "Civil Law"

At the outset, any ambiguity about the meaning of the word **civil** must be dispelled since it controls and determines the nature of the body of law which is contained in a **civil code**.

---

1. Linguistic reason also: The Louisiana Civil Code is the only contemporary civil code to be written in English and not translated into English. There exists a 2013 translation of the French Civil Code on the site of Legifrance.

INTRODUCTION

The word **civil** has undergone a substantial metamorphosis over the centuries before appearing in the titles of "Le Code Civil des Français/the French Civil Code" and the "Louisiana Civil Code" in the early 19th century. When we look back at the origin of the word civil, we find its root in the Latin word **civis**, which means "citizen." The law of the Roman citizen was then called the **jus civile** or "civil law" in contrast with the law applicable to the "peregrinus" or foreigner, which was the law of nations or jus **gentium**.

In his Institutes, the jurist Gaius was writing that, "That law which a **people establishes for itself is peculiar to it, and is called ius civile (civil law) as being the special law of that civitas** (State), while the law that natural reason establishes among all mankind is followed by all peoples alike, and is called **ius gentium** (law of nations or law of the world) as being the law observed by all mankind."[2] We find the same basic definition in Justinian's Institutes: "*#1. Civil law is distinguished from the law of nations, because every community governed by laws uses partly its own and partly the laws which are common to all mankind. That law, which a people enacts for its own government, is called the civil law of that people ... #2. Civil laws take their denomination from that city in which they are established: it would not therefore be erroneous to call the laws of Solon or Draco the civil laws of Athens: and thus the law which the Roman people make use of, is styled the civil law of the Romans.*"[3] Centuries later, "during the centuries of feudalism, public and private law became merged and it is only with the rise of the sovereign state in the sixteenth century that they again became separate. They have always remained so."[4] Thus **private law** or **civil law** prevailed in countries which had inherited the Roman law tradition as distinguished from another body of law known as public law. Subsequently, with the growth of commercial law, or the law of merchants, the words **civil law** were to apply to that part of the local private law applicable to persons in general. This is the sense given to the expression **civil law** today, as illustrated by the French and the Louisiana Civil Codes.[5]

---

2. Zulueta, Francis. *The Institutes of Gaius: Part I-II.* Clarendon Press, 1946, p.3.

3. Thomas Cooper, *The Institutes of Justinian*, Philadelphia 1812, Lib.I,Tit. II De Jure Natuarli, Gentium, et Civili.

4. F.H. Lawson, *The Thomas M.Cooley Lectures Fifth Series*, University of Michigan, 1953, p.89.

5. See Julio Cueto-Rua, *The Future of the Civil Law*, 37 LA.L.REV.645 (1977).

2. The Meaning of "Code" in the Expression "Civil Code"

Several meanings have been given and are still given to this word "code." History teaches us that the original Latin meaning of "code" is **codex**, like the **Codex** of the Emperor Justinian of 534 AD. A **codex** was a manner of presenting a written legal text in another manner or form than a roll of papyrus. When legal texts on papyrus were rolled together they formed a **volumen** or volume. In a **codex**, on the other hand, layers of papyrus were folded and bound together from the back in the form of a **codex**, very much like a book we are using today. A codex was, therefore, a form of material support for a legal text and, at the same time, a measure of length of the texts bound in the format of a codex. We will find, in the history of the civil law, a private codex put together by Gregorianus, and another such **codex** compiled by Hermogenianus in the 3rd century. There were also, of course, official compilations of legal texts made under the direction of some emperors, like the most influential Codex of the Emperor Theodosian in the 5th century or the best known of all the **codices**, the **Codex** of the Emperor Justinian in the 6th century. Thus, the first original meaning of **codex** was merely a material form of binding documents together under one cover. It was a method of compiling and presenting texts of laws on a variety of topics under a single cover.

The word "code," as we understand it today, has a very different meaning as well as a distinct portent. Today a code is much more than a material form of presenting a text. From a formal point of view a code is, as described by Cornu's *Dictionary of the Civil Code*, a "collection of laws; more precisely, an official collection of legislative and regulatory provisions governing a specific field (ex. Penal Code, Civil Code …) often with an indication of the country of origin (ex. Italian Civil Code, Swiss Code of Obligations)." However, most typically, when examined from a scientific viewpoint, "a code is a consistent body of rules governing a specific field, body of legal rules in a given field, stemming from the compilation and arrangement of rules relating to it (usually according to a systematic organization); however, it may turn out to be a codification in the true sense or a purely formal and clerical codification."[6] In the same vein, the Private Law Dictionary of the Québec Research Centre of Private and Comparative Law describes a code in these terms: a "body of fun-

---

6. Cornu, *Dictionary of the Civil Code*; entry: code.

damental legislative provisions designed to present the subject matters of an important branch of law in a systematic and coherent manner."[7]

3. The Path to Grasping the Sense of the Law of a Civil Code

Taking as a basic, even though not fully accurate, assumption that a "civil code" is a specific feature of a civil law jurisdiction,[8] we must explore the reasons why "civil code" and "civil law" appear to go hand in hand. These reasons are found in the centuries old history of the birth and growth of the civil law. As will be obvious from this survey of the history of the civil law, particular attention will be given to the original and specific process of **codification** as opposed to "legislation." We hope to make it clear that **codification**, as an original method or, rather, a unique art of drafting rules of law as sources of law, cannot fulfill its raison d'être without the support and assistance of two other sources of law, which are "jurisprudence/case law" and "doctrine/scholarly writing." A "civil code" cannot be a living reality and enduring statement of the written law it contains without these two necessary and indispensable partners who cooperate with the legislator in the making of the civil law. The law of a civil code is a "tripartite" creative and working process.

After these three sources of law have been described not only in their unique and necessary coexistence but also, and more importantly, in their "solidary" working relationship within a codified system of law, we will be in a position of drawing the conclusion that they are indispensable, one to the other two, in the same manner as are the three sides of an isosceles triangle. To illustrate this working relationship we will describe and illustrate the many methods of interpretation and reasoning that are used by the courts and doctrine so as to "grasp the true sense of the laws, apply them in a discerning fashion and supplement them in those cases which the laws have not provided for."[9] It is there that we will find the key to the "fertility" of a civil code and the reason for the long and still continuing existence of the French and the Louisiana Civil Codes.

---

7. Québec Research Center of Private & Comparative Law, *Private Law Dictionary and Bilingual Lexicons*, Les Editions Yvon Blais Inc., 1991, 2nd edition.

8. Greece was a civil law country and jurisdiction before it adopted its Civil Code of 1950; Scotland is a mixed jurisdiction with civil private law but no code.

9. Alain Levasseur, "Code Napoléon or Code Portalis?" XLIII Tul.L.Rev., 1969. p.771.

Part I

The Making of a Civil Code

A "civil code" is a particular form of expression of the legislator's will and a particular kind of statute; therefore, we will focus in Part I on the different types of sources of law and on the institutions, public and private, that play a role, essential or accessory, in contributing to the formulation, expression and implementation of these sources of law. History will reveal that many of the major sources of law and institutions that shaped Roman law into a legal system will find their twin sources of law and institutions in contemporary civil law systems. We will establish also that the unquestionably scientific writing style of some Roman jurists, such as Gaius or Ulpian, was the precursor of the process of "codification," which marked the early 19th century in France and Louisiana.

Chapter 1

Historical Developments of Sources of Law and Law Making Institutions

A. From the Code of Hammurabi to the XII Tables: The Beginning

One of the first, if not the first, written (engraved, actually) listing of royal edicts that is known to have existed before the XII Tables is the so-called *Code of King Hammurabi* of the second millennium BC. Hammurabi was king of Assyria in Mesopotemia and from his throne in the city of Babylon he undertook, over a time span of twenty-five years, to unify the whole region of Mesopotemia which he turned into an empire. The "Code" itself is in the form of a stele (one such stele is now in the Louvre Museum in Paris), which was most likely engraved, over a period of time, during Hammurabi's reign between the years 1792 and 1750 BC. This "code" was not a "code" in the contemporary understanding of the word as it included many edicts, which did not concern legal issues. An interesting feature of the Hammurabi code is that it was written in the vernacular language of the empire, in a simple language that could be understood by all who could read from the stele displayed in public places. It goes without saying also that Hammurabi's code deals with "reality," with factual issues and ignores abstractions. Centuries later Napoléon will instruct the four members of the commission charged with drafting the French Civil Code to write a code in a language that a layperson, a farmer in particular, could understand without the help of "counsel."

It is of interest to give here two examples of legal rules, which will sound very familiar to civil law lawyers:

A: If someone wants to hand over to someone as a deposit silver, or gold or whatever else, all that he wants to hand over he must display in front of witnesses and he will draft a contract; then (and only then) he will hand over it in deposit.

B: If someone has leased an ox or a donkey and if, in the countryside, a lion killed it, it is a matter for the owner exclusively.

If someone has leased an ox and if he caused its death because of negligence or beating, he will give to the owner of the ox an identical ox.[10]

[**Comment:** the combination of the limited space available to the drafters with the need to instruct the reader as practically and efficiently as possible, leads to the important observation that: the first law cited above is made up of a statement of fact, starting with "If" and ending with "whatever else," and a rule of law starting with "all that he wants ..." and ending with "in deposit." The same is true about the second "law": the facts are included in that part of the sentence starting with "If someone ..." and ending with "killed it," and the law then is "it is a matter for the owner exclusively." This observation will be made even more forcefully when we explain the process of "Codification" and when we explain some Methods of Interpretation. In other words, already in the Code of Hammurabi we can observe a beginning of the process of codification that will flourish in the 19th c.]

B. From the XII Tables to the Corpus Juris Civilis (CJC): Sources of Law

1. From the XII Tables to the Classical Period of Roman Law

History and tradition tell us that Rome was founded by Romulus and Remus, sometime around 753 BC. The Latins and the Sabines had settled in Latium, a hilly area on which Rome was built, hence the name "Romans." Following Romulus, six kings were to succeed each other until some kind of revolution led the patricians in 509 BC to rise against the monarchy and to replace

---

10. *Le Code de Hammurabi*, Introduction, traduction et annotation par André Finet, *Les éditions du Cerf*, Paris, 2004.

it with a republic or, in Latin, "Res Publica," public thing. The patricians, few in number compared to the plebeians, made up what we could call the "aristocracy." As such, they enjoyed privileges in conjunction with or because of the wealth they had. On the other side of the social ladder, the plebeians made up the larger group of citizens. They were poor in comparison with the patricians. In addition they were deprived of privileges and, by and large, enjoyed very little legal protection.

The applicable law at that time was a customary law, therefore an unwritten law, which was transmitted orally from generation to generation. A "college" of patricians, the *Pontiffs*, administered the customary law through their own interpretation of what they considered to be the prevailing and appropriate customs. Since the *Pontiffs* were patricians, the plebeians were of the firm belief that the patricians/pontiffs were administering the customs in a manner mostly biased and prejudicial to their interests as the lower class of citizens. Inevitably, a conflict arose and resulted in the plebeians being granted some political rights, such as the right to hold their own assemblies. These assemblies, known as the *concilia plebis*, were empowered, at an early stage, to issue laws or *plebiscita*, only for the governance of their constituents, the plebeians or *plebs*/the common people.

As a result of a forceful political campaign that started in 462 BC and that was led by officials of the *concilia plebis*, the patricians consented to the creation of a college of ten men (*decem viri*) charged with incorporating the customs in some written form for all to be able to see and, therefore, to have knowledge of. A first set of 10 "*panels*" or "*tables*"[11] were displayed giving to the plebeians a new "**jus**" or set of laws. However, because these first 10 Tables were considered unfinished and incomplete, two additional *tables/panels* were subsequently added. Once the XII Tables were finally engraved or drafted, the assemblies of the people (*comitia*) passed a law to make the XII Tables the first piece ever of any legislation being adopted by the people. It marked the beginning of legislation becoming a source of law for the citizens, the citizens of Rome in this case.

The raison d'être of the XII Tables, the purpose for which they had been forced upon the patricians, was to formally recognize that the citizens had some rights and, more importantly, to grant them some means of having these rights enforced. Here are two examples of "laws" from the XII Tables:

---

11. Likely made out of wood or possibly of stone or bronze; it is not really known because the original Tables were likely destroyed when Rome was sacked and burned by the Gauls in 387 BC.

A: If he (plaintiff) summons him (defendant) into court, he shall go. If he does not go, (plaintiff) shall call witnesses. Then only he shall take him by force. If he refuses or flees, he (plaintiff) shall lay hands on him. If disease or age is an impediment, he shall grant him a team (of oxen). He shall not spread with cushions the covered carriage if he does not wish to.

B: When a debt has been acknowledged or a judgment has been pronounced in court, 30 days must be the legitimate grace period. Thereafter, arrest of the debtor may be made by the laying on of hands. Bring him into court. If he does not satisfy the judgment (or no one in court offers himself as surety on his behalf) the creditor may take the debtor with him. He may bind him either in stocks or fetters, with a weight of no less than 15 lbs. (or more if he desires). After 60 days in custody, the case is returned to the court, and if the debt is not then paid, the debtor can be sold abroad as a slave, or put to death.[12]

[Comment: the same observation can be made about these two laws of the XII Tables as was made, and even more so, about the Code of Hammurabi. For example, in law B above, one *statement of facts* starts with "when a debt" and ends with "in court" and the *rule of law* applicable to these facts is that "30 days must be the legitimate grace period," as well as, "thereafter, arrest of the debtor may be made by the laying on of hands." Again, we are presented here with a broad *statement of facts*, since the debt can be of any source, such as a contract, a delict/tort, followed by the applicable *rule of law*. We can see, in the XII Tables, a precursor of the process of codification that will take place in the 19th century.]

a. The Praetor

In 367 BC a new source of law, **praetorian law**, emerged. By legislation the institution of the **Praetor urbanus**, or **Praetor of the city** (urbs), was created. Because of the size of the city of Rome and the extent of its population, several **Praetors** had to be installed. Although all equal in name, the **Praetor maximus** and the **senior praetors** enjoyed some privileges of seniority over the **junior praetors**. In terms of ranking among the several kinds of magistrates who were governing the city of Rome, the **Praetor** occupied the second rank behind the **Consuls** from whom the **Praetor** took over the handling of the court's business. The **Praetor urbanus** or urban Praetor, who could be a plebeian, although not trained in the law, was responsible for the overall operation of the judicial system. In this capacity he was specifically in charge of the administration of the **jus civile** or the law that applied between Roman citi-

---

12. http://www.csun.edu/-hcfll004/12tables.htm.

zens. Upon assuming his functions for one year, the **Praetor**, who was vested with the "jurisdictio imperium," would promulgate an **edict**[13] wherein he would lay down the list of remedies he would grant during his tenure. Since the Praetors succeeded each other every year, it became customary for a new Praetor to include in his list of remedies all or most of the remedies granted by his predecessors. As a consequence, the list of remedies would grow with every new Praetor until **Hadrien**, in 130 AD, instructed the jurist **Julien** to issue a consolidated version of all the edicts under the form of the "*Perpetual Edict*" (edictum perpetuum).

The **Praetor** was in charge of the first phase of the litigation, the **in jure** phase. The Praetor's task was to delineate the parameters of the particular type of action brought before him. The parties would appear before the praetor to lay out the facts of their claims and defenses. Not being trained in the law, the praetor would be assisted by a "*jurist*" who was a *legal scholar* but not an advocate in the sense that an advocate would be involved in the actual conduct of a court case on the side of a party. The function of the praetor was to declare the law (*ius dicere*) in a "*formula*" which was like a program or directive by means of which the praetor would select a judge (*judex*) and instruct that judge as to the solution that he should adopt in the case. Such was the "*formulary procedure*."[14] "*Most remedies were concerned with recognized claims ... [H]owever the praetor could grant a formula in a situation in which there was no precedent. Officially in such a case he was not making new law; that would have been beyond his powers. In effect he was saying that the claim justified a remedy and so the law must provide it. Although he spoke as if he were just implementing existing law, he was in fact making new law ... It enabled the praetor to grant a deserving party a remedy, when he felt that the popular sense of justice required it, while at the same time maintaining the formal integrity of the civil law ... The law derived from the grant of the new remedies, contained in the*

---

13. **edictum** from the **jus edicendi.**

14. A formula was made of four parts: the "*demonstration*" was laying out the facts of the case in a very succinct manner: a line or two. Then came the "*intention*," which was the claim made by the plaintiff who would assert, for example, that he was the owner of something or creditor of someone. The third part of the formula was the "*adjudication*," which was a statement instructing the judge to rule in favor of one party or the other. Again, a very short statement. Then came the "*condemnatio*," which was that part of the formula giving the judge the power to sentence or exonerate a party to the case. For example: the praetor would tell the judge, "sentence X to pay Y this amount of money; however, if it appears to you that X does not owe that amount, exonerate him." The *judex* would then act accordingly.

edicts of the praetors, was known as **ius honorarium** *(from the honores held by elected office holders). Most legal development affecting civil disputes in the second half of the Republic was achieved through this kind of law.*"[15] All in all, the edicts became important instruments of legislation in developing the judicial process in parallel with the legis actio of the ius civile.

As regards the **judex** he was a layperson originally selected from among the patricians. Every year the praetor would publish a list of names of some three hundred **judices** identified as "good persons." As a matter of principle, the judex was chosen by the parties themselves as they looked at litigation as a very personal and sensitive matter, hence the name of "arbiter" often given to the judex. If the parties could not agree on a **judex-arbiter**, a judex was selected either by lot or the praetor would submit to the parties several names of judices until the parties agreed on one. Once chosen or selected, the judex had to accept to be the judex in the case. Trials were open to the public and usually held on the forum or in an assembly, **comitium.** When the parties were one a citizen and the other a foreigner-**peregrinus**, as was often the case in the provinces, the judex was often called by another name: **recuperator** or **reciperator.** Since, in this instance, there would likely be a conflict of law, the law of the citizen or **jus civile** on one side, and the law of the foreigner or **jus gentium** on the other side, the judex would be selected from the country of the defendant.

With the territorial expansion of Rome and its hegemony around the western Mediterranean area, the number of non-citizens grew to the point of requiring that a special body of law be applied to them, the *ius gentium,* and administered by another praetor than the praetor urbanus. In 242 BC, the office of **praetor peregrinus**, or praetor for the foreigners or residents of the provinces (**peregrini**), was created. The law that this praetor administered was made up of some Roman law with some elements of foreign legal systems. Because of its great flexibility and greater maturity than the *ius civile,* the *ius gentium* or law of nations, became applicable to Roman citizens as well as to non-citizens. In the words of Peter Stein, "*the 'law of nations' was sometimes characterized as natural law* (**ius naturale**). *It came to be accepted that the law of nations and natural law were similar, except for the institution of slavery ... Neither the praetor nor the iudex, nor the advocates who represented the parties before them, were trained in the law and all of them needed expert help from time to time.*"[16]

Two observations can be made here. The first observation is that there is much similarity between the roles of the praetor and the iudex acting in tan-

---

15. Peter Stein, *Roman Law in European History*, Cambridge, 1999, p.9–12.
16. *Idem*, p.13.

dem in Roman law and the role of the courts, the judges and the jurists in filling up the so-called gaps in the law of the Civil Codes of France and Louisiana, as we shall explain below. The second observation is that there is much similarity between, on the one hand, the merger of the *ius civile*, as a set of rigid forms of actions or *legis actiones*,[17] with the *ius edicendi* or *praetorian law* developed by the praetor and, on the other hand, the origin of the *writ system at common law* which became a rigid system of actions until it merged eventually with "equity" as created by the Chancellor of England, who acted very much like the Roman praetor and its formulary system.[18]

b. Legislative Bodies and Forms of Legislation

During the Monarchy (about 753 to 509 BC), what we would call "law" today was in the hands of the pontiffs, who were mostly concerned with sacred law and family law. Around the 450s BC, as seen above,[19] the XII Tables became the first written statement of laws in Rome. Later on the **Senate**[20] was essentially composed of patricians until the end of the 4th century when it was opened to the most outstanding plebeians. The Senate issued **senatus consulta,** which, until the emperor Hadrien, were more statements of advice to the praetors than actual pieces of legislation. When Hadrien became emperor, the *senatus consulta* will be given the force of law.

Besides the *XII Tables* and the *senatus consulta*, there existed another source of law under the form of **lex**.[21] The **lex** was voted upon and adopted by assemblies or comitia of the Roman people. There were different kinds of *comitia* corresponding to different groups of people. The *comitia centuriata* gathered together Roman citizens on the basis of their being divided on account of their wealth, in "centuries" or one-hundreds. The structure of the

---

17. They became "gradually unpopular" among early makers of law for their excessive technicality. It was carried so far, that a party who made the slightest mistake would lose his case. Consequently, they were abolished by the L.Aebutia and the two Ll. Iuliae and litigation by means of adapted pleadings, that is, by formulae, was established. *The Institutes of Gaius* by Zulueta; III De Actionibus Law of Actions.

18. On the common law, see Theodore F.T. Plucknett, *A Concise History of the Common Law*, 5th edition, Little Brown and Company, 1956; See also John H. Langbein et. al, *History of the Common Law: The Development of Anglo-American Legal Institutions,* Aspen Publishers, Wolters Kluwer, 2009.

19. Supra p.5 et seq.

20. From "Senatus," the council of the elders, the Senate; cf. Theodor Mommsen, *History of Rome*, Wildside Press LLC, 2008; "Senex," according to *A Latin Dictionary* by Charlton T. Lewis and Charles Short (Oxford, 1995): old, aged, advanced in years.

21. Plural: leges.

comitia tributa reflected a division of the citizens on the basis of the territory of a district or *tribus*, tribe. By the year 241 BC, there existed four urban districts or tribes and thirty-one rural districts. Later on the membership in a tribe became hereditary. A third form of comitia was the *comitia curiata,* which seems to have been concerned with matters of wills and family law, particularly adoption. As far as the *concilium plebis* is concerned, it started as an assembly of the plebeians and provided for the plebeians. The *concilium plebis* acted under the leadership of its representatives, the **Tribunes,**[22] who were elected for a one-year term and required to act by common consensus as a "college." It was then that the principle of "collegiality" emerged, for the first time, as a form of government. Until 287 BC, the enactments passed by the *concilium plebis*, the **plebis scita,** were binding on the plebeians only. The lex Hortensia of 287 BC gave the force of law to the **plebis scita** over all the Roman citizens, whether plebeians or patricians. An important piece of legislation passed by the *concilium plebis* in 287 BC, the **Lex Aquilia** became the foundation of the law of delicts as found in the French and Louisiana Civil Codes.[23]

c. *"Juris-Prudentia": "Knowledge of the Law": Doctrine*

In the early history of Rome, until about 300 BC, only patricians could become pontiffs and, as such, they were in charge of all legal matters, including the ability to give legal advice. Things changed with the election of the first plebeian pontiff in 253 BC. Still, the pontiffs had somewhat of a free rein to interpret the laws, often to suit their own purposes. Beginning around the year 200 BC the first lay practitioners of the law will come on the scene and take on the specific title of "juris-consultus," meaning learned, skilled, in the law.

What was known in Roman law as **juris-prudentia** is, today, what we refer to as legal scholarship, doctrine, legal writing or the work of those wise in the law, knowledgeable in the law. These laypersons skilled in the law or **juris-consultus,** i.e., jurisconsult or jurist, gave *consultations* on issues of law to those, litigants or not, who would call on them. The jurist was asked to respond by rendering an opinion. By contrast, the Roman **advocatus** was handling a case for his client before the praetor and judex. Interestingly enough, advocates were not allowed to receive fees from their client, as they were assumed to provide their services to the community rather than to their client!

---

22. From two, to four and then to six of them.
23. Fr. Civ. C. art. 1382 et seq; La. Civ. C. art.2315 et seq.

Because of the fundamental role played by the jurists in Roman law ever since the second century AD, and because jurists will have an equally fundamental role in the making of the civil law from the 11th–12th centuries AD, starting with the "**glossators and commentators**" in Italy, we must elaborate a little on this unique institution of the **jurist** in the civil law tradition as it stands in sharp contrast with the common law tradition.

"The main agency of legal development in the classical period […] was the literature produced by the jurists, both those in the imperial service and those conducting a private practice. The jurists as a class were favoured by the emperors; already Augustus (27 BC–14 AD) granted certain jurists the right to give opinions with the emperor's authority,[24] *perhaps in order to relieve the pressure created by the demand for rescripts*[25] *from the imperial chancery. A century later Hadrian (c.117–138 AD) laid down that if the opinion of all the jurists with this right were in agreement what they held was to have the force of a lex. What this means is not clear, but it may well refer to a practice that had grown up of citing as precedents juristic opinions given in similar cases in the past. The jurist-law of the classical period was marked by certain characteristics, which may be summarised as follows. First, there was a continuous succession of individuals, all dedicated to the law and each familiar with and building on the efforts of his predecessors, whose views they cited, especially when they agreed with them but sometimes when they disagreed. Secondly, they alone could be said to have a comprehensive knowledge of private law … Thirdly, the jurists were concerned with the day-to-day practice of the law and could recognise when modifications or reform of the rules were needed … Finally, they enjoyed complete freedom to express divergent opinions."*[26]

This classical period of Roman law saw the publication of major works by some of the most prominent jurists whose writings will be incorporated in the *Corpus Juris Civilis* of the emperor Justinian in the 6th century. *"The classical period reached its climax, in the decade after the Constitutio Antoniniana, [in 212] in the work of three jurists whom later ages were to consider the most distinguished, Papinian, Paul and Ulpian. Each of them held the highest imperial office, that of praetorian prefect, and was both the emperor's principal legal officer and his chief of staff. They all wrote prolifically on the law. Papinian excelled in the analysis of particular cases and his solutions to legal problems show a keen*

---

24. Called: *jus respondendi ex auctoritate principis;* hence: *responsa.*

25. Rescripta were replies to petitions or requests for instructions addressed by private individuals to imperial officials.

26. See Stein supra note 15 at p.16–17.

moral sense and a desire to reach a just result. Paul and Ulpian are known for their great commentaries, which synthesised the work of their predecessors and passed it on in a mature, but still very complex form, to later generations."[27]

The best-known and most influential work of that time was authored by **Gaius**, a law teacher who lived under the reign of Marcus Aurelius. Gaius's "*Institutes*" are an impressive systematization of Roman law, very much like an introductory work for law students. Actually, later on and for the same reason, Justinian will instruct his commission to draft a book for law students which he will also call "*Institutes*." In his "First Commentary" in his *Institutes*, **Gaius** displays a remarkable grasp of the complexity of the law by managing to represent it in an original, comprehensive and, yet, concise format of divisions of concepts decreasing in scope and breadth, thereby leading logically and systematically to lesser divisions which themselves lead to even lesser subdivisions. A uniquely creative form of drafting the law was born in the hands of Gaius and other jurists, and it is that same form of writing the law that we will find in 19th-century Europe in the hands of other jurists charged with "codifying" the law of France and Louisiana in particular. Indeed, Gaius's technic of drafting and legal methodology will influence the scientific process of codification in the countries of the European continent. However, as we will see later on, this process of codification will not cross over into the island of England thus creating one of the most fundamental identifiable features distinguishing the civil law from the common law.

As examples of Gaius's drafting technic and legal methodology, let us consider the following excerpts from his Institutes:[28]

(*Commentarius Primus*) 1. "*Every people that is governed by statutes and customs observes partly its own peculiar law and partly the common law of mankind. That law which a people establishes for itself is peculiar to it, and is called ius civile as being the special law of that civitas (State), while the law that natural reason establishes among all mankind is followed by all peoples alike, and is called ius gentium as being the law observed by all mankind. Thus the Roman people observes partly its own peculiar law and partly the common law of mankind. This distinction we shall apply in detail at the proper places.*" Then, further illustrating the newly created style of making and writing the civil law in as a structured, comprehensive and, yet, as clear and simple a style as possible, Gaius lists in one single introductory sentence "all" the sources of the civil law of his

---

27. See Stein supra note 15 at p.20–21.

28. Francis de Zulueta, *The Institutes of Gaius*, Oxford at the Clarendon Press, 1946, p.3.

time: 2. *"The laws of the Roman people consist of leges, plebiscites, senatusconsults, imperial constitutions, edicts of those possessing the right to issue them, and answers of the learned. A lex is ... A plebiscite is ..."*

A comparison with the Louisiana Civil Code is most instructive: **Article 1.** *The sources of law are legislation and custom.* **Article 2.** *Legislation is a solemn expression of legislative will.* **Article 3.** *Custom results from practice repeated for a long time and generally accepted as having acquired the force of law ...*

(Commentarius Secundus) "1: Things ... are subject either to divine right or to human.... 10: Things subject to human right are either public or private. 11: Public things are regarded as belonging to no individual, but as being the property of the corporate body. Private things are those belonging to individuals. 12: Further, things are divided into corporeal and incorporeal. 13: Corporeal things are tangible things.... 14: Incorporeal are things that are intangible, such as exist merely in law, for example an inheritance, ... obligations however contracted."

We find some interesting similar articles in the Louisiana Civil Code: **Article 448.** *Things are divided into common, public, and private; corporeals and incorporeals;* **Article 461.** *Corporeal are things that have a body, ... Incorporeals are things that have no body, but are comprehended by the understanding, such as the rights of inheritance, ... obligations, ...*

More examples:

From Gaius's Institutes:[29]

"#70. Alluvial accretions to our land become ours, again by natural law. That is held to be an accretion by alluvion which a river adds to our land so gradually that it is impossible to estimate how much is being added at any particular moment. #71. Accordingly, if a river tears away a piece of your land and carries it down to mine, that piece remains yours. #72. But if an island arises in the middle of a river, it is shared by all the riparian owners on either side of the river; if, however, it be not in the middle of the river, it belongs to the riparian owners on the nearer side."

Consider the following articles from the Louisiana Civil Code: **Article 499.** *Accretion formed successively and imperceptibly on the bank of a river or stream ... is called alluvion. The alluvion belongs to the owner of the bank ...* **Article 502.** *If a sudden action of the waters of a river or stream carries away an identifiable piece of ground and unites it with other lands on the same or on the opposite bank, the ownership of the piece of ground so carried away is not lost. The owner may claim it within a year, or even later, if the owner of the bank with which it is united*

---

29. *Idem* p.83.

*has not taken possession. **Article 503.** When a river or stream, ... opens a new channel and surrounds riparian land making it an island, the ownership of that land is not affected.*

We will borrow our conclusion on this first period of Roman law that spread from the XII Tables to the end of the classical period in the 3rd century, from E.Metzger: *"A comparison between a Roman magistrate's power to innovate and the historical equity jurisdiction of the English Chancellor is unavoidable. In many respects the distinction between the state law and the honorary law resembles that between the common law and equity in England. But there is less to this resemblance than first appears. The Roman magistrate presided over both types of action and therefore, as Buckland says, 'We shall not find in the Roman law a system of rules developed gradually by a permanent tribunal whose function it was to give relief which for any reason could not be obtained in the ordinary courts.' Also, when we consider that some of the innovations introduced by the praetor out of a desire for equity would then be memorialized in his edict for future cases, the praetor resembles more a legislator than a chancellor. Finally, it is a fair argument that the greater source of equity in Roman law is not the praetor but the jurists, whose innovations would be felt principally in the second trial phase of a lawsuit."*[30]

2. Post-Classical Period to the Corpus Juris Civilis (3rd to 6th Century)

When Diocletian became emperor in 284 AD, the Empire was so widely spread over southern Europe and the whole Mediterranean basin that it became most difficult to govern it all from one single place. Diocletian first planned to divide his Empire into a Western Empire, with Rome as the seat of its government, and an Eastern Empire with another capital which, initially, was called Byzantium and was renamed Constantinople after the emperor Constantine I who ruled from 306 to 337 and built the city. *"The reign of Constantine [will mark] another major change in the Roman empire, namely the emergence of Christianity as an officially tolerated religion. The emperor having himself been converted to the faith, he promulgated legislation making the faith lawful as in the Edict of Milan of 313.... Christianity becoming the official religion of the empire under Theodosius I in 378. This step had considerable influence upon various departments of the law, particularly marriage, inheritance and*

---

30. Ernest Metzger, "Actions," in *A Companion to Justinian's Institutes*, New York: Cornell University Press, 1997, p. 20.

parental power."[31] The actual division of the Empire took place in 395 after the death of the emperor Theodosius. *"This severance of the mainly Greek speaking east from the Latin west was to have momentous consequences in later centuries."*[32] During the Dominate, the emperor being "**Dominus,**" imperial legislation became a most important and prolific uniform and unifying source of law applicable from one end to the other of the empire. As a consequence of the substantial amount of imperial legislation, compilations had to be undertaken. Among the earliest compilations were the *Codex Gregorianus* (in 291), which included imperial constitutions dating back to Hadrian, and the *Codex Hermogenianus* (in 295), which included imperial constitutions promulgated between 293 and 294. *"Both Gregorius and Hermogenian ... produced during the reign of Diocletian ordered collections of imperial legislation, in the main rescripts to assist those seeking to determine what the law was on a particular matter. Both works are called codices, not because they are codes in the modern sense of systematic, comprehensive legislation on a whole area of the law, but because they were written on individual sheets of parchment bound together in book form and not on papyrus as hitherto had been used.... Neither has survived in its entirety; ... Both were independent productions; they were not in any sense official collections and had no legislative force ... There is evidence that both works were subject to some updating after their initial completion, and in the case of the Hermogenianus this continued into the second half of the fourth century."*[33]

"During the fourth century, the call to enhance the clarity and accessibility of the law became ... louder. Many [responsa and rescripta] were mutually contradictory and there was often doubt as to what should not be regarded as authoritative ... The emperors of the Dominate took initiatives themselves to compile the law and establish what they considered to be authoritative sources of law. They also wanted to bring the huge legacy of classical jurists within their orbit. Emperor Constantine was the first to promulgate legislation granting formal authority to certain works by classical jurists while imposing a prohibition on the use of other works (321 AD). A hundred years later, in 426, the Eastern Roman emperor Theodosius II and Western Roman emperor Valentinianus jointly promulgated the 'Law of Citations.'"[34] This "Law of Citations" stated that from now on the works of only five jurists could be cited in courts. They were: Paul, Ulpian, Papinian,

---

31. Thomas Glyn Watkin, *An Historical Introduction to Modern Civil Law,* Ashgate, 1999, p.61.

32. See Stein supra note 15 at p.23.

33. Thomas Glyn Watkin, *An Historical Introduction to Modern Civil Law,* Ashgate, 1999, p.57 et seq.

34. Randall Lesaffer, *European Legal History,* Cambridge Uni. Press, 2009, p.108–109.

Gaius and Modestinus. When reaching the point of having to decide, the judge had to add the concurring or somewhat identical opinions of these jurists and the majority of the same opinions was to become the law of the case. In the event the opinions were divided on the same issue and no majority view could be ascertained, the judge was instructed to adopt Papinian's opinion as the law of the case. Should the judge be left with no relevant opinion at all or where, in the absence of an opinion from Papinian, two identical opinions were pitted against another set of two other identical opinions, the judge was then free to decide as he saw fit.

[**Comment**: it is important to remember the role of these writers for their contributions to the judges' decisions but also, and primarily, for their contributions to "legislation." We will see below how important legal scholars are to the growth of the civil law under the form of civil codes but also to the development of the courts' decisions.]

A most important work for the study of the Roman law of the 4th and 5th centuries AD is the promulgation, in 438, of the Codex Theodosianus by the emperor Theodosius II. Eight jurists worked together for nine years, starting in 429, to compile this Codex.[35] The Codex was divided in sixteen books and included the imperial constitutions promulgated by the emperors Constantine to Theodosius II, or sixteen emperors and some one hundred and twenty six years of legislation.[36] The Codex Theodosianus contains rules mostly on public law and ecclesiastical law. With this Codex, Roman law was contained in the form of a text, which, because it had become accessible, was considered as the exclusive source of law for the type of law it covered. Between the time of the publication of this Codex and the next major compilation of Roman law by the emperor Justinian, the "new constitutions" or "*novellae constitutiones*" promulgated by the emperors were added chronologically to the Codex.

With the beginning of the 5th century the western empire gradually fell under the control of Germanic tribes coming from the north. Under their pressure, the emperor Honorius transferred the western capital from Milan to Ravenna. The Visigoths (or western Goths) entered Italy under the leadership of **Alaric** sacking the city of Rome in 410, while the Saxons were invading

---

35. It is worth pointing out the small size of the commission that put together the Codex Theodosianus, as it will be also a small commission of four that will draft the French Civil Code and a "commission" of two that will draft the Louisiana Civil Code of 1808 and a commission of three that will draft the Louisiana Civil Code of 1825.

36. R.De Fresquet, *Traité Elémentaire de Droit Romain*, Paris, p.26.

Britain. Very quickly, the Visigoths moved also across into Gaul, settling in the southwest part of France and further south in Spain. They established their capital in Toulouse. On the eastern side of Gaul, the Burgundians settled their capital in Worms, while the Ostrogoths (eastern Goths) occupied some parts of southeastern France, as well as parts of Italy. By the year 476 "*the last Roman emperor in the west gave up his throne and the Germanic kingdoms in Gaul and Spain became independent ... To some extent the vacuum created in the centre of the western empire by the collapse of imperial government was filled by the Church ...*"[37] With the fall of the Western Roman empire in 476, the imperial capital was in fact moved to Byzantium in the East.

Following the fall of the Western Roman empire, some of the rulers of the Germanic tribes undertook to enact different codes of law, written in Latin, not only for the Roman citizens who had remained but also for their own Germanic peoples who had settled in the newly conquered territories. The first of these so-called "barbarian codes" was the *Edictum Theodorici* of King **Theodoric**, king of the Ostrogoths, issued around 460 in the southwest part of France. This Edict borrows substantially from Roman law, particularly from the *Codex Gregorianus*, the *Codex Hermogenianus* and the *Codex Theodosianus* which had had in use in the West. The same *Edict of Theodoric* incorporated also writings by classical jurists such as Paul, Papinian and Gaius, which could be found in prior promulgations of Roman law, such as the *Law of Citations*. In 506 King **Alaric II**, king of the Visigoths, promulgated a code of law known as the *Lex Romana Visigothorum* or *Breviarum Alarici*. This "Breviary" is also a form of vulgarization of Roman law consisting in an abbreviated rendition of the *Theodosian Codex*, some imperial constitutions and a simplified version of *Gaius' Institutes*. Another Germanic code was promulgated under the name of *Lex Burgundionum* by King **Gundobad** for the kingdom of the Burgundians on the Rhône. "*The Visigothic Roman law is our main source for western vulgar law in the last century of the western empire. It also became the main source for Roman law in the kingdoms which replaced the empire from the sixth century to the eleventh. It was in force in the Visigothic kingdom of Spain until the middle of the seventh century, when the fusion of the two peoples was recognized and the law became territorial, applicable to all living in the kingdom, rather than personal. In practice the Visigothic collection also maintained its authority in the kingdom of the Franks which, after their defeat of the Visigoths in 507 and of the Burgundians in 532, extended over the whole of former Gaul. The Franks accepted the 'personality principle' but published no compilation of Roman law, preferring*

---

37. See Stein supra note 15 at p.30.

instead to use the Visigothic and the Burgundian Roman law, which were often copied together in Frankish manuscripts."[38]

C. From the Corpus Juris Civilis to the "Civil Codes"

1. From the Corpus Juris Civilis to the 12th Century

While the western empire was "falling," the eastern empire was flourishing under the reign of its emperor Justinian, a learned and versatile man, an energetic commander of its armies, an art lover and a highly skilled administrator. Justinian was determined to restore the ancient Roman empire to its former grandeur, and he intended to return Roman law to the prestige it had known just a few centuries before his reign. Justinian surrounded himself with efficient and learned ministers and administrators to carry out his ambitious plans. A year after he had become emperor in 527, Justinian ordered that a Codex containing the still relevant constitutions of his predecessors be put together. He appointed a commission of ten jurists among whom were Tribonian, Julian, and Theophilus. Working quickly, within one year the commission published the *Codex Justinianus* in 529. This Codex was a compilation[39] of selected "Constitutions," thereby suggesting that the commission had the authority to resolve conflicts and to change the law where necessary so as to replace the existing "Codicis."[40] Later, this first *Codex* will take on the name of *Codex Vetus*, as it was replaced by a new Codex in 534, which included the many new constitutions promulgated by the emperor since the first Codex of 529.

The following year, Justinian instructed an enlarged commission to undertake a major innovative endeavor in legal literature: the codification of the writings of the classical jurists. Six commissioners, under the leadership of **Tribonian**, were joined by civil servants. Justinian, as Napoléon will do later on, was very involved in this monumental work. Here are some examples of the instructions he gave the commissioners: "*#4. We order you to read and revise the books dealing with Roman law, written by those learned men of old to whom the most revered emperors gave authority to compose and interpret the laws so that the whole substance may be extracted from them, all repetition and discrep-*

---

38. See Stein supra note 15 at p.32.

39. From the Latin "*compilare*," meaning to "plunder."

40. Plural of codex; *A Latin Dictionary*, Lewis and Short, Oxford, 1955.

ancy being as far as possible removed, and out of them one single work may be compiled, which will suffice in place of them ... #5. It is necessary to set it out in a most handsome work ... and to distribute the whole law into fifty books and distinct titles, in imitation both of our Codex of constitutiones (enactments) and of the Perpetual Edict, in such a way as may seem convenient to you, so that nothing may be capable of being left outside the finished work already mentioned, but that in these fifty books the entire ancient law—in a state of confusion for almost fourteen hundred years, and rectified by us—may be as if defended by a wall and leave nothing outside itself ... #6. Out of a large number of authors, you must not make a judgment that the work of one is better and more equitable, since it may happen that the opinion of one writer, perhaps of inferior merit, is better at some point than those of many other authors, even superior ones ... ; but if you perceive that anything taken from them is necessary to supplement or interpret the works of Papinian, that man of supreme ability, you must not hesitate to set this down too as having the force of law.... #11. We therefore command that everything is to be regulated by these works: the Codex of constitutiones (enactments) and the other law clarified and arranged in the book that is to be. There may be added something else promulgated by us, serving the purpose of Institutes, so that the immature mind of the student, nourished on simple things, may be the more easily brought to knowledge of the higher learning. #12. We command that our complete work, which is to be composed by you with God's approval, is to bear the name of **Digest** *or* **Encyclopedia.** No skilled lawyers are to presume in the future to supply commentaries thereon and confuse with their own verbosity the brevity of the aforesaid work, in the way that was done in former times, when by the conflicting opinions of expositors the whole of the law was virtually thrown into confusion."[41]

[Comment: we will see further down that Napoléon will also forbid legal scholars to express their opinions on the provisions of "his" Civil Code for fear that their writings would bring about the "end" of his newly enacted Civil Code.]

The commission completed this work of the Digest in the record time of three years with the promulgation of the Digest in December 533. *"According to the promulgation act, the collection comprised some 150,000 lines, while the commission had read three million lines in 2,000 scrolls. In total, excerpts from the works of thirty nine jurists have been preserved, of which texts written by Ulpian account for about 40 per cent."*[42] The Digest is divided into fifty books,

---

41. *The Digest of Justinian*, Vol.1 Mommsen, Krueger Watson Editors, University of Pennsylvania Press, 1985, p.XLVII–XLIX.

42. Randall Lesaffer, *European Legal History*, Cambridge, 2009, p.111.

which are then sub-divided into titles that contained, on particular topics, excerpts from the writings of the jurists of the classical period.

The size and complexity of the Digest were such that law students would have had a difficult time navigating through it. With this in mind, the emperor had his commission prepare an elementary book on the law of the Digest so that the students would not be deterred by the study of this most important subject matter:

> "The Emperor ... Justinianus, ... to the youth desirous of studying the law, greeting. 3. We summoned the most eminent Tribonian,.... together with the illustrious Theophilus and Dorotheus, professors of law, all of whom have on many occasions proved to us their ability, legal knowledge, and obedience to our orders; and we specially charged them to compose, under our authority and advice, Institutes, so that you may no more learn the first elements of law from old and erroneous sources, but apprehend them by the clear light of imperial wisdom; and that your minds and ears may receive nothing that is useless or misplaced, but only what obtains in actual practice.... 4. ... we directed that these Institutes should be divided into four books, which might serve as the first elements of the whole science of law.... 6. These four books of Institutes thus compiled, from all the Institutes left us by the ancients, and chiefly from the commentaries of our Gaius ... and also from many other commentaries, were presented to us by the three learned men we have above named. We read and examined them, and have accorded to them all the force of our constitutions. 7. Receive, therefore, with eagerness, and study with cheerful diligence, these our laws ..."[43]

As regards the style and structure of the provisions of the Digest and the Institutes, they were so much the product of an original, skilled and creative legal science that, as we shall see below, they will have a determinant impact on the future "codifiers" of the 19th century. As illustrations of this unique style and structure of the provisions of the Institutes as they were taken from the writings of "jurists" of the classical period of Roman law, we have selected the following:[44]

> #1. Civil law is distinguished from the law of nations, because every community governed by laws, uses partly its own and partly the laws which

---

43. *The Institutes of Justinian* with English introduction, translation and notes by Thomas Collett Sandars, M.A., Gaunt, 1997, p.73–75.

44. *The Institutes of Justinian* with notes by Thomas Cooper, Esq. Philadelphia 1812.

are common to all mankind. That law, which a people enacts for its own government, is called the civil law of that people. But that law, which natural reason appoints for all mankind, is called the law of nations, because all nations make use of it. The people of Rome are governed partly by their own laws, and partly by the laws, which are common to all men …

#3. The Roman law is divided, like the Grecian, into written and unwritten. The written, consists of the plebiscites, the decrees of the senate, ordinances of princes, the edicts of magistrates, and the answers of the sages of the law.

#9. The unwritten law is that, which usage has approved: for daily customs, established by the consent of those who use them, put on the character of law.

[**Comment**: for comparison purposes, we have cited La. Civ. C. Articles 1 to 3 above at p. 19. It is worth stressing here the fact that both in the Institutes of Justinian and the Louisiana Civil Code there are, fundamentally, two broad sources of law, which are classified as "written" and as "unwritten." In both the Institutes and the La. Civ. C., the "written law," under its different forms, is the expression of governmental institutions and, as such, "written law" prevails over the "unwritten law." Notice that in the Institutes "the answers of the sages of the law" are considered as being a source of "written law." In the French Civil Code, custom is not mentioned and for both historical and "constitutional" reasons, custom is not a source of law.

The following additional illustrations[45] are given not only because they are the product of the skilled work of Justinian's commission in the 6th century, but also because they bear a great resemblance with the work of Gaius (2nd century AD) as we intentionally included it above.[46]

Institutes: #20. Moreover, that ground which a river hath added to your estate by alluvion, becomes your own by the law of nature. And that is said to be alluvion, which is added gradually, that on one can judge how much is added at each moment of time.

La. Civ. C. art. 499. Accretion formed successively and imperceptibly on the bank of a river or stream … is called alluvion. The alluvion belongs to the owner of the bank.…

---

45. *The Institutes of Justinian* with English introduction, translation and notes by Thomas Collett Sandars, M.A., Gaunt, 1997.

46. Supra p.11.

Institutes: #21. But, if the impetuosity of a river, should sever a part of your estate, and adjoin it to that of your neighbour, it is certain such part would still continue yours; but if it should remain for a long time joined to the estate of your neighbour, and the trees which accompanied it take root in his ground, such trees seem, from the time of taking root, to be acquired to his estate.

La.Civ.C.art. 502. If a sudden action of the waters of a river or stream carries away an identifiable piece of ground and unites it with other lands on the same or on the opposite bank, the ownership of the piece of ground so carried away is not lost. The owner may claim it within a year, or even later, if the owner of the bank with which it is united has not taken possession.

"Justinian's legislative efforts may be regarded as a genuine codification. His ambition consisted of collecting and sifting the entire amalgam of legislation, case law and jurisprudence and replacing it with one great collection. Anything that did not appear in his new collection was abolished. The Justinian collection was the only source of law. It laid claims to exclusivity and completeness ... Justinian's codification explicitly built on a millennium of legal tradition. It was a reorganization of Roman law, not a radical reform. In terms of later legal development, the Justinian collection acted as a conduit for transmitting the achievements of one thousand years of legal development to later generations. The rediscovery of the Justinian Digest in the eleventh century sparked off the advent of legal science in western Europe."[47]

The *Corpus Juris Civilis* marked the end of an era in the long and highly constructive history of Roman law, just as the emperor Justinian intended. At the same time the *Corpus Juris Civilis* symbolized the consolidation of Roman legal system in the 6th century and served as the foundation for the "civil law system" in the centuries beyond the 11th century. Most importantly, this consolidation of Roman law under the form of the Digest had been entrusted to legal scholars, including law professors, in particular, who had written down the law in Latin as ordered by Justinian. The Latin language was the language of the learned and educated whereas the Greek language was the language of the general population of the Eastern Empire. To reach the general population it became necessary to reproduce, in a Greek translation, parts and excerpts of the *Corpus Juris Civilis* and to frame these excerpts under the form of easily accessible statements that the people could understand. These efforts resulted in trimming, pruning and simplifying the Digest and in transcrib-

---

47. Supra note 42 at p.112–113.

ing it into some form of written law. An example of such a "Greek" legislation is the *Basilica* (imperial law), which was started during the reign of the emperor Basilius Macedo (867–886) and completed by his son, Leo the Wise (886–911). Two additional works on the *Corpus Juris Civilis* were promulgated, the *Procheiron* (a manual of law) and the *Epanagoge* (an introduction to law). Much later, Constantine Harmenopulos published the *Hexabiblos* (1345), which survived the rule of the Turks (1453) and became the official source of statutory law of the Kingdom of Greece in 1835. It was followed by the Greek Civil Code of 1946. Thus, Roman law survived in the Eastern part of the empire albeit in the Greek language rather than in its original Latin version.

2. From the 12th Century to the Era of Codification

In the West, following the collapse of the Western Roman Empire at the hands of Germanic tribes, the destiny of Roman law found a new breath of life at the end of the 6th century in northern Italy and the southern part of France. Strangely enough it did not occur under the form of the survival and, even less, of an implementation of Justinian's work but, rather, through a collection of barbarian compilations of law. *"The earliest of these barbarian laws is the Edict of Theodoric, ... issued circa 460 ... It is a simplified version of passages drawn from the codes of Gregorius, Hermogenian and Theodosius II.... Its Roman law is so lacking in sophistication compared with the originals and the subsequent work of Justinian that the Roman law it exemplifies has become known as vulgar Roman law."*[48]

King Alaric II of the Visigoths (484–507) compiled a code of law known as the *Breviarum Alaricianum or Breviary* of King Alaric and also as *Lex Romana Visigothorum*. The major reason that prompted the barbarian kings to implement these codes of law was to allow their Roman subjects to continue to live under the legal system that had been theirs until then, i.e., Roman law. The Germanic population lived under its own law or customary law, with each tribe living under its own particular law. It is interesting to point out that, already at that time, custom was made up of two complementary elements: a material or factual element and an intellectual or psychological element. The factual element consisted in a series of identical practices or cases (usus) lasting over a period of time leading to the intellectual or psychological element, which created the common belief that the factual element was binding because dic-

---

48. Thomas Glyn Watkin, *An Historical Introduction to Modern Civil Law*, Ashgate, 1999, p.70.

tated by the law or *opinio juris*.[49] Thus the authority of law attached to custom was based on tradition.[50]

The revival of industry, commerce and banking in 12th-century Italy brought about a change in the life of the cities and a need for schooling. Universities[51] as a place of higher learning were created around four disciplines: medicine, theology, canon law and civil/Roman law. Universities blossomed all over Europe: Salerno, Rome, Perugia, Padua, Pavia ... in Italy; Montpellier, Paris, Toulouse, Orleans ... in France; Salamanca, Valencia, Huesca ... in Spain; Oxford and Cambridge in England. *"The mediaeval jurists were ... following their classical predecessors in fixing their sights upon the explication of a text, but in doing so they gave this tradition a new stimulus and a fresh impetus, which was destined to present the world eventually with the legal codifications of the nineteenth and twentieth centuries ..."*[52]

At Pavia, Roman law was studied mostly in its vulgar form of the *Lex Romana Visigothorum*. The rediscovery of the *Digest* at the end of the 11th century offered the students a structured text to study. The interest was more in identifying the sources of Roman law and the purpose of the law in general than in engaging in an in depth interpretation of the *Digest* itself. Still, in a certain manner the school of Pavia pointed the way to a new approach to the study of legal texts. *"Jurists were no longer satisfied simply with making summaries of texts. They now wanted to interpret them in depth. Where adherence to the letter of a text would lead to injustice, the Expositio stressed that its rationale, the ratio legis, must be identified and the text understood in the light of that ratio.[T]he honour of producing the first expositors of Justinian's compilation belongs not to Pavia but to Bologna."*[53] The Digest came to be considered as **ratio scripta**, or written reason.

The beginning of the study of the *Digest* at the school of Bologna is due mostly to **Irnerius** (c.1055–1130) who adapted the new scholastic method of analysis in his scrutiny of the *Digest*. The technique consisted in writing explanatory notes or *glossae* to provide a logical interpretation of the provisions of the *Digest*. The *glossae* were written, first, in between the lines, above or under the words. As the amount of *glossae* grew to incorporate additional ex-

---

49. On the component part of a custom, see La. Civ. C. art. 3: "Custom results from practice repeated for a long time and generally accepted as having acquired the force of law. Custom may not abrogate legislation."

50. See *Dictionary of the Civil Code*, LexisNexis, 2014; word: coutume.

51. From *universitas*, a gathering of professors and their students.

52. See Watkin supra note 48 at p.83.

53. See Stein supra note 15 at p.45.

planations, they could no longer fit in between the lines; they were then moved to the margins of the manuscripts. Some *glossae* were short comments, giving a simple explanation or clarification of the law, whereas others were elaborate material explanations of the law.[54]

The glossators undertook a comprehensive analysis of the *jus civile* and strove to provide a logical and coherent interpretation of the Roman law of the *Digest*. "*For the Glossators up to the middle of the 13th century, Roman law was the law of a universal empire. They studied it and taught it as such to students who came from all over Europe to Bologna to study according to what would later be called the mos italicus. In this way, their methods of studying and teaching Roman law quickly spread throughout Europe*."[55] However, their analysis, being essentially a textual analysis of the Digest, could neither be more logical nor more systematic that the text of the *Digest* itself.[56] As *glossae* were added to *glossae* from one generation of scholars to another generation, this cumulative writing of layers of *glossae* resulted in a somewhat confusing and overwhelming "commentary" on the *Digest*. The end result was the integration of all the glossae under the form of one single work known as the *Glossa Ordinaria*, the *Ordinary* or *Standard Gloss*. This *Glossa Ordinaria* by the glossator **Accursius** (c.1184–c.1263) consists in a huge compilation of all the glossae written on the *Corpus Juris Civilis*. It was the crowning of years of work by the glossators demonstrating thereby their full mastery of *the Corpus* of Justinian. In addition, the *Glossa Ordinaria* was used in the practice of law. It referred to the sources of law, which were attached and provided an interpretation and an explanation with the addition of cross-references. In the universities, the *Glossa Ordinaria* became a teaching instrument because, among other features, it presented solutions to practical legal problems and filled many gaps in the text of the *Corpus Juris Civilis*. Judges in particular relied much on the Glossa as it gave them an authority to rely on so that their opinions would have a sound and well established legal foundation.

The Bologna school engendered several other types of legal writings, which can be analogized to contemporary forms of legal discourse. The "*summae*" were like commentaries on a particular title or several titles and even on the *Corpus Juris Civilis* itself. In this instance such commentaries amounted to legal

---

54. When several glossae were grouped together on a part of the Corpus, this collection of glossae was referred to as "apparatus," the ultimate example being the *Glossa Ordinaria* of **Accursius**.

55. Cappelletti, Merryman, Perillo, *The Italian Legal System*, Stanford University Press, 1967, p.21.

56. The legacy of Irnerius was continued by some of his disciples and pupils, among them the famous four doctors: Jacobus, Martinus, Hugo and Bulgarus.

treatises as treatises are known today in civil law jurisdictions. A "*casus*" was somewhat like a "case-note" meant to explain a text on the basis either of a real case or of an hypothetical case. Such an exercise in writing case-notes is still thriving today in civil law jurisdictions under the pen of jurists, such as law professors, judges or attorneys.

There existed also a form of writing known as "*quaestiones.*" *Quaestiones* were raised after the exposition of legal developments so as to present possible solutions to difficulties encountered in some parts of the *Digest*. Some *quaestiones* could take the form of a dialogue of a scholastic nature between a student and a "doctor" of the law. Another type of legal writing of some fame was under the form of summaries or "*summae.*" The author of a *summa* would write the law in the form of a general rule, he would devise concepts and give their definitions thereby stating a rule of law that would go much beyond practical situations. The best known *Summa* is **Azo's** *Summa Codicis* which stated the Roman law of the Digest in the form of a "*code.*"[57]

At the same time, the Church continued to mingle with Roman law. After the collapse of the Empire in the West and the conquest of the German tribes, Rome remained the seat of the Papacy. In the 6th and 7th centuries, the Popes strengthened the unity of the Church and issued a series of papal "decretals" while councils of bishops issued decrees or canons. All through the 7th century and beyond, Latin was, in Italy, the language of education, the language of the Church and of written documents. Education was mostly dispensed in monasteries. The works of the "Fathers" of the Church, like Saint-Augustine (354–430) or Saint Gregory the Great (540–604), were the main objects of learning and collections of the decisions taken by bishops councils were put together.

---

57. "In the early 12th century there is evidence of the acceptance of the new Bologna learning across the Alps in south west France. This area, Provence in its wider medieval meaning, including Languedoc and the Dauphine, was a fertile ground for such influence. The regional customs contained more Roman elements derived from the Visigothic and Burgundian collections of Roman law, than the customs of other regions … Civil law was also taught in schools founded in Toulouse and Orleans … In England, teaching of the new legal learning is associated with the Lombard **Vacarius** who was recruited from Bologna in the 1140s by Archbishop Theobald of Canterbury. As more universities were founded, it was accepted that law in a university setting meant the study not only of the local customary law but of civil and canon law. These were the only forms of law which had the universal character expected of a university discipline. Indeed no European university offered instruction in the law of the land until the 17th c. As a result, in every European country a university-trained lawyer was necessarily a Roman lawyer. Such lawyers came to share a common legal culture, based on the same texts, expounded in the same language, Latin." See Stein supra note 15 at p.55–57.

"The main custodian of the Roman legal tradition was the Church. As an institution, the personal law of the Church throughout Europe was Roman law ... As the problems facing the Church increased in complexity, so the references to Roman law increased ... The Roman material relevant to the Church was brought together in particular collections, such as the 'Lex Romana canonice compta' of the ninth century ... In the tenth and eleven centuries, the equilibrium postulated by Pope Gelasius' principle of two separate authorities (or the doctrine of the two swords representing the two powers), vested in the Pope and in the emperor, was disturbed by the struggles between the Church and the Empire ... Halfway through the eleventh century, the papal Curia embarked upon its own reform of the church, known as the Gregorian reform after Pope Gregory VII (1073–84). One of the focal points of the reform was the struggle to wrestle the church from secular, and especially imperial, control. More specifically, the conflict turned on the role played by the emperor in the appointment to higher church offices ... Gregory VII himself denied the emperor the right to invest bishops and abbots with the symbols of their office (investire) ... With the Gregorian Reform, the papacy assumed the leading role in ecclesiastical reform and extended it to the whole clergy ... The Gregorian Reform put an end to the co-operation between the two heads of Christianity—the emperor and pope ... The doctrine of the two swords transferred by Christ to those in authority on earth ... became established in canon law through the Decretum Gratiani (c.1140), the most important collection of canon law of the Middle Ages ... This Decretum was more than just a simple collection of texts relevant to canon law; the author also immediately applied the scholastic method to his textual material ... By introducing a hierarchy for the sources and by the use of scholastic dialectics—especially the distinctio—Gratian sought to arrive at unequivocal answers to the issues raised.... Gratian laid the foundations for a jurisprudence of canon law. Among other things, he introduced elements of Roman jurisprudence into such law. His book acquired great authority throughout Europe and became the basic text for the academic study of canon law. The book was the subject of study at the schools of canon law established in Bologna and elsewhere in Italy and Europe. In the same way that the Corpus iuris civilis was disclosed by the glossators, Gratian's own work was glossed. The standard gloss, the <u>Glossa Ordinaria</u> of the <u>Decretum Gratiani</u>, was that of Johannes Teutonicus (c. 1245). The great period of papal legislation had had not yet commenced in 1140. In the two centuries after Gratian, popes and councils produced a mass of new laws. Selective collections of the new rules were put together in various phases ... The first of these collections of decretals was the <u>Liber decretalium Extra decretum vagantium</u> (Book of the decretals outside the Decretum) or for short the <u>Liber Extra</u> ... The <u>Liber Extra</u> consisted of five volumes. The next supplement was consequently given the name <u>Liber Sextus</u> (1298 ...) In 1314, under Clemens

V, there followed the <u>Constitutiones Clementinae</u> and in 1325, the <u>Extravagantes</u> *of John XXII. All these texts, from the <u>Decretum Gratiani</u> to the <u>Extravagantes</u> plus a number of minor supplements and corrections, were amassed in 1582 into the <u>Corpus Iuris canonici</u>, the code of canon law. This continued to apply until it was succeeded in 1917 by the first <u>Codex iuris canonici</u>, which in turn had to give way to the new <u>Codex</u> of 1982.*"[58]

The Italian legal scholars or doctors of law who were writing in that period of time between the completion of Accursius' *Glossa Ordinaria* and the middle of the 14th century have been referred to as **Post Glossators**. The French jurists who, at the same time, were writing also on the Roman law of the *Glossa Ordinaria* and the *Corpus Juris* were called the "Ultramontani," because they were located on the other side, the French side, of the Alps mountains. At the University of Orléans, the ultramontani Jacques de Revigny and Pierre de Belleperche planted the seeds of a new school, which will become the school of the **Commentators**. The Ultramontani were of the view that the *Glossae* needed to be analyzed and written about, hence the writings of "*comments*" on the *Glossae* themselves. In their lectures, the Ultramontani would not hesitate to take their distance from the written text of the Gloss to find guidance and inspiration in Aristotle's philosophy and doctrine which they mixed with the Christian writings of Aquinas. They used a dialectical form of reasoning to strengthen the logic of their reasoning and to build their legal analysis by analogy on the **ratio**-reason of a text. "*Reason*," from then on, will be given a dominant role in the formulation of legal rules and in solutions to be given to practical problems. The foundation and creation of the **jus commune** were emerging.[59]

Cinus, one of the most prominent Italian commentators, came from Orléans (France) and settled in Bologna where he introduced the "comment" approach developed by the Ultramontani. His most illustrious student was **Bartolus** of Sassoferrato, professor at Pisa and Perugia. After Bartolus' death in 1357, the legal scholars who belonged to the <u>school of the commentators</u> took on the name of "**Bartolists**." Bartolus wrote a substantial commentary on Justinian's work providing a complete discussion of all the parts of the *Corpus Juris*. "*Under his influence the study of the civil law became less purely academic and more oriented towards the legal problems of the day. He and his followers ...*

---

58. See Lesaffer supra note 42 at p.202–265.

59. Whereas the glossators were mostly interested in the study of words, the commentators were concerned with the "reason" behind the law. Hence, below, our survey of methods of interpretation and reasoning based on "words" and "reason."

sought to find in the texts rules, which would be appropriate for late medieval so-
ciety but would still carry the authority of imperial law ... Bartolus' most distin-
guished pupil was Baldus de Ubaldis who dominated the second half of the 14thc.
He commented not only on the civil law but also on canon law and feudal law
and perfected the 'opinion' (consilium), a discussion of the legal issues raised by
a particular case. This form of legal literature completed the adaptation of the
civil law to contemporary problems."[60]

The commentators elaborated a theory according to which local statutes
ought to be interpreted against the background of what was to become the *jus
commune* so that the interpreted statute would deviate as little as possible from
that *jus commune*. Feeling free to apply the law to the circumstances of their
times whenever it was reasonable and acceptable, the commentators eventually produced the *jus commune* which was instrumental in spreading Roman
law all over western Europe in the 15th and 16th centuries. *"They were able to
present Roman law (in the shape which it assumed under their hands) in the light
of a natural law founded on scientific principles, a law, therefore, which claimed
to be recognized as a common law valid not only for Italy, but for all countries. In
a word, the Commentators raised Roman law for the second time in history to the
rank of a universal law."*[61]

These academic jurists *"began to express opinions as to what the underlying
principles and system of the **Corpus Juris** suggested should be the answer to questions for which the text itself did not provide. If the text revealed an answer, that
was accepted as beyond question to be the law, but if the text did not reveal an
answer, the trained reasoning of the jurists could express an opinion, which while
not of the same authority as an answer revealed by the texts, was nevertheless of
some persuasive value ... Thus, alongside the authority of texts, there developed
as in ancient Rome a subsidiary authority attaching to the opinions of those
learned in the law, what was to be called by modern civil lawyers, **doctrine** ... The
civil law was thus extending beyond the limits of the texts once more in order to
adapt itself to the needs of the contemporary world."*[62]

[**Comment**: these historical developments will be very relevant as they will play
a constructive role in the nature and foundation of the methods of interpretation we will be considering below. It will be particularly true as regards the
methods of interpretation calling upon the "reason" or "ratio" on which a

---

60. See Stein supra note 15 at p.71–74.

61. Rudolph Sohn, *The Institutes, A Textbook of the History and System of Roman Private Law*, 2nd ed., Oxford, 1907, p.155.

62. See Watkin supra note 48 at p.95–96.

statute or code articles are grounded. It will become apparent that what the Glossators and even more the Commentators were doing in the 12th to 15th centuries will be duplicated in the 19th century and still today. Notice also the creation of the "case-notes" and "comments on cases." Note also the statement by Watkin: "alongside the authority of texts, there developed as in ancient Rome a subsidiary authority attaching to the opinions of those learned in the law, what was to be called by modern civil lawyers, **doctrine** ..."]

At the same time the school of the Commentators was making a name for itself, the humanist school was also penetrating the legal world of the *Corpus Juris*. It established itself in Universities in France mostly, and Bourges in particular which became, in 1464, the main center of learning of legal humanism. The approach of the humanist scholars was to return to the texts of the *Corpus Juris* stripped of all the *glossae* and comments that had been built around it. The jurists of the humanist school brought an historical approach to the study and interpretation of Roman law. To better understand Roman law, the humanists directed their interest to learning more about the Roman society and about the social context that contributed to the writing of the *Corpus Juris*. The greatest legal humanist scholar was Jacques Cujas who studied most carefully the *Florentine manuscript of the Digest*[63] believed to be the older and closer version to the original of the Digest. For **Cujas**, to better understand the Digest one had to balance the reading of the Florentine manuscript against the **ratio juris** or the legal principle that justifies and helps explain the rule. The humanists recognized that the state of Roman law was related to the state of the Roman society and that as society changed so did the law.

"Most of the humanists recognized that, for rational and equitable solutions to many perennial problems, the work of the classical Roman jurists was unrivalled. They felt free, however, for the first time to criticise the form in which those rulings were transmitted ... Neither the Digest nor the Code has a rational order and they contained many repetitions and antinomies ..."[64] For the commentators, *"[B]ecause Roman law was perfect and timeless, ... it should provide an appropriate solution to any current legal issue. The result was that the commentators interpreted and reinterpreted Roman law fairly freely until it provided a solution to the issue in question. In fact, they subjected Roman law to the needs of practice ... The humanists regarded the ancient Roman law sources not as authorities but as evidence of the best legal system man had ever devised. Roman law mer-*

---

63. Located and preserved today in the Laurentian library in Florence.
64. See Stein supra note 15 at p.79.

ited study as a model, an example … [T]he humanist jurist had to go beyond the study of Roman law. He himself had to discover and articulate the best legal system for his own age. Roman law formed the most important source of information to that end but could not be adopted literally as it stood … The key question was no longer, 'What does Roman law say? or 'What is the ideal law?' but 'What would be the best possible law in these circumstances?'"[65]

[**Comment**: one can assert that the humanist school had an impact on the influence of Roman law it developed out of the schools of the Glossators and the Commentators. It re-directed the study of law from the study of "Roman law," as such a study of law is a "science," looking at law as any other scientific discipline that can be presented in a logical and rational order, in the sense of going from the general to the particular. Such is the nature of the civil law today. Indeed *"the underlying beliefs of the Civil law jurists and professors of law, and of lawyers, judges … is that law is 'scientific law' because: (a) law is an object susceptible of scientific knowledge; it constitutes the proper object of the so-called science of positive law; (b) law is created by means of technical procedures based on scientific knowledge; (c) law is taught by means of scientific concepts and propositions. The civilian jurist is interested in the intellectual mastery of legal phenomena."*[66]

In France, the collections of Roman law made by the Barbarian kings had resulted in the southern part of France becoming a country of "written law" or *"pays de droit écrit,"* in contrast with the northern part of France where customary law prevailed so that the northern part of the territory became known as "pays de coutumes." However, Roman law had some persuasive authority in the *"pays de coutumes"* whenever customary law was silent on some legal issue. Furthermore, Roman law was taught in all Universities whether located in the South or the North of France. Still, the customs were many and varied, some very broad in their territorial application, whereas many others had very limited scopes of application. For political reasons the kings of France made it very clear that the Crown was the official source of law and that Roman law had no greater authority than a custom. The basic reason why the French kings would take this "political" position towards Roman law was that to receive Roman law as a primary source of law would have meant the recognition of the political supremacy of the Holy Roman Empire,[67] as well the acceptance

---

65. See Lesaffer supra note 42 at p.354–355.

66. Julio Cueto-Rua, *The Future of the Civil Law*, 37 La L.Rev. 645, at p.646, 1977.

67. Holy Roman Empire: "As early as his victory at Lechfeld in 955, Otto the Great, in the tradition of the Roman generals, was declared <u>imperator</u> by his troops. Until his coronation by the pope in 962, his claim to the title of <u>imperator</u> was based on the fact that, like

of its legal system, namely the *Corpus Juris Civilis*. Thus, Roman law came to be considered as a secondary source of law and French local customs had primacy over Roman law.

Nevertheless, because Roman law was considered as "written reason" (**ratio scripta**), Roman law was an available source of legal information that could be used to supplement or modernize the customs of northern France, as illustrated by the Roman law of obligations, a field of law on which customs had very little to say and on which, on the contrary, Roman law was very elaborate and systematic.

In the *pays de droit coutumier*, more or less the northern two-thirds of the country, hundreds of customs prevailed. Many of these customs were *"coutumes locales"* or special customs for cities and even villages. Other customs, less in number, were referred to as *"coutumes générales"* because their scope of application was wider, sometimes a whole province like the *coutume de Normandie* or the custom of *Bretagne-Brittany* and, most importantly, the *coutume de Paris*. This large number of "oral" customs, and their overlap, created much confusion and uncertainty as these customs were mostly "personal" to an individual as long as he lived in the territory of his custom. But customs were also territorial in the sense that any local lord or sovereign of a territory would look upon the application of a custom from another territory or locality as an infringement upon his own sovereign rights. Thus, customs could not be enforced outside the territory under their control and over which they had gained legal authority through the ages.

By and large, these many customs, or this customary law, consisted in a variety of combinations of Roman law, Germanic rules and customs, Canon law and usages. To attempt to remedy this confusing and intricate web of customs, Charles the VII issued an ordinance of major importance, as times will prove: the *"Ordonnance de Montils-les Tours"* of April 1454. This ordinance called for the customs to be written down in official compilations. By the end of the 15th century and throughout the 16th century a selection of the more important customs, some sixty general customs and three hundred local customs, were committed to writing. Printing made it possible to pub-

---

Charlemagne, he ruled over various peoples ... The emperorship came with the crown of the old _regnum Italiae_, to which the German kings had laid claim since the tenth century. Thus, it became the monopoly of the German kings ... During the course of the eleventh century, the emperors started to style themselves as 'Roman' emperors, and even as 'Roman' kings of Germany. In 1254, the name 'Holy Roman Empire' was used for the first time." Randall Lesaffer, *European Legal History*, Cambridge, 2009, at p.221.

lish these compilations for all to see and read the written laws of the Kingdom of France. The *custom of Paris* was compiled in 1510 and revised in 1580; the *custom of Brittany* was compiled in 1539 and revised in 1580 as well. The revisions were due, essentially, to the involvement of judges and jurists. Once published with the King's approval and his sanction, a custom acquired the authority attached to written law and was to be observed like a statute.

[**Comment**: as opposed to many of the customs of England that became part of the unwritten common law administered by the courts and judges in England from the 12c. onward, the customs of northern France were written down in compilations made by jurists and judges alike; as written law these customs were like statutes ... and not "court-decisions" or "cases."]

After the customs were written down in the 16th and 17th centuries, the texts of these customs could be studied, comparisons could be made and general principles could be identified. Treatises and commentaries on the written customs soon appeared under the pen of jurists like **Dumoulin** (1500), **Loysel** (1536–1617), **Coquille** (1523–1603) ... On their side, Courts, particularly the *Châtelet de Paris* and the *Parliament of Paris* (Parlement de Paris) simplified and unified the customary law to the point of making the custom of Paris the dominant custom. Among the jurists of the later part of the 1600s and 1700s who will also have a great influence on the Civil Code of France (1804) and the Civil Codes of Louisiana (1808, 1825) are Jean **Domat** (1625–1695), Robert Joseph **Pothier** (1690–1772) and H.Fr. **D'Aguesseau** (1668–1751).

[**Comment**: **Dumoulin** wrote an extensive "*Commentaire de la coutume de Paris*," 1538; Coquille wrote an "*Institution au droit français*"; **Domat** wrote a major work "*Les lois civiles dans leur ordre naturel.*" **Pothier** wrote numerous treatises, most notably a treatise on "*Obligations*"; **D'Aguesseau**, as Chancellor, had a series of ordinances passed on "gifts, inheritance, wills." All these works, and more, will become very helpful in the process of codification in the early 1800s.]

"Several of the leading jurists of the period functioned as magistrates in the courts of France, including the <u>Parlement</u> de Paris. Decisions of the <u>parlements</u> were recorded and published during these centuries, witnessing to the role which interpretation in the courts played in harmonizing the various customs into a national law. It is clear from both the works of the jurists and the reports of the decisions of the <u>parlements</u> that, although the French customs were regarded as the chief source of law in the courts together with royal enactments, considerable use was also made of concepts and even of rules derived from Roman civil law. In particular, the method of reasoning employed owed much to the style which had been

developed in relation to the civilian sources in earlier times. The <u>Parlement</u> of Paris also had the right to be informed of royal legislation and to request the king to think again concerning it if it was not happy with the proposal. This power of making a <u>remonstrance</u> was specifically recognized in the <u>Ordonnance</u> of Moulins, 1566" [which also regulated the means of proof in matters of contracts].[68]

Many "Ordonnances" or ordinances, were adopted by the kings of France and registered with the Parliament of Paris to become the laws of France. For example, the *ordonnance de Villers-Cotteret* (1539) introduced in the royal courts a criminal procedure modeled after canon law; the *ordonnance de Blois* (1579) regulated the formalities of marriage. Under the reigns of Louis the XIVth and Louis the XVth, important *ordonnances* were issued in matters of civil procedure (1667), overland commerce (1673), maritime commerce (1681), donations (1731), wills or testaments (1735), and substitutions (1747). These *ordonnances* will become important guides and sources for the writing of the French Civil Code of 1804 and the French Code de Commerce, or Commercial Code of 1808.

In Spain, the Arab conquest of 711 brought an end to "Visigothic Spain." However, the *Lex Romana Visigothorum* established a body of Roman law to which was added the new Germanic law. From the 13th century to the 15th century, Spain was divided into a multiplicity of kingdoms and principalities, so much so that there was no uniform law in existence.

"Within the Christian kingdoms that gradually took form, very diverse factors were active. First, the 'Fuero Juzgo' (formerly known as Forum or Liber Iudicum, meaning: Book of the Judges or Province of Judges) whose text suffered interpolations and modifications. This Liber Iudicum of the Visigoths, termed eventually as Fuero Juzgo in Castillian, was in force between 600s and 1000s. Second, the 'Lex Romana Visigothorum' which in some districts retained influence as representing the pre-Justinian Roman tradition; a great mass of Germanic customs ... Third, the incursive bodies of pre-feudal and true feudal law, especially in the north and northeast; and lastly, land allotment charters, town fueros ... which constituted the local or cantonal legislation of seigniories and municipalities ..."[69]

Spanish students were attracted to Italy and attended the teachings of the glossators, **Irnerius** in particular at the University of Bologna (between 1088 and 1125) and the commentators even after the creation of the University of Salamanca in 1239. King Ferdinand of Castille and Léon commissioned the

---

68. See Watkin supra note 48 at p.123.
69. *The Continental Legal History*, vol. 1, Boston, 1912, p.583–607.

translation into the vernacular of the *Fuero Juzgo*. His son Alfonso X, or Alfonso the Learned, had a compilation of law prepared under the name "*Especulo (Espejo) de todos los Derechos,*" or "*Mirror of all the Laws.*" However, this compilation never materialized. Some time later, the same Alfonso launched a much larger compilation, which was destined to a great future, known as "*El Libro de las Leyes.*" Because *El Libro de las Leyes* was divided into seven parts, it became better known as "*Las Siete Partidas.*" Started in 1256, *Las Siete Partidas* were completed in 1265. The sources of *Las Siete Partidas* were the many *Fueros* and customs of Castille and Leon. Among them there were the *Fuero Juzgo*, the *Fuero Real* or Royal custom, the *Canon law* and the works of the Roman jurisconsults in combination with the works of the Italian commentators. "*Las Siete Partidas, at first, met political opposition in areas where custom was strong. Only in 1348 by the Ordenamiento de Alcala was it promulgated as general law by Alphonso XI; it was general law subordinate to particular custom …*"[70]

"*By the beginning of the 1500s, Spanish law was already substantially formed … Its history from that time to the opening years of the 1800s consists … in an accentuation within the civil law of the Romanist influence … A compilation in nine books of 'ordenamientos' of Cortes and royal orders named the 'Nueva Recopilación' was published and promulgated in 1564. In the practice of the courts, and particularly in civil law, more favor was enjoyed by the scientific Roman system. Legal science was one of the most extensive and most intensely cultivated fields of Spanish learning in the 1500s and 1600s (Vives and Suarez were two of the greatest philosophers of the age) … and the extensive participation by the legists-Romanists in political life, as well as the frequent consultation by the kings of the learned members of the clergy, were other powerful influences in the development of legal studies … The 1700s were an age of great reforms in the social and political life of Spain. The causes lay in the influence of France and in the great spirit of the times, which throughout Europe was propitious to innovations and progress … During the 1700s, the Nueva Recopilación were re-edited five times, each time adding a part … of the new legislation. Years later approval was given to the project of another compilation which rearranged that of the year 1567 and all its supplements into twelve books, and was printed in 1805 under the title of 'Novissima Recopilación de las Leyes de España' … The 1700s constituted in Spain an epoch of flowerage in legal studies … chief among the Romanists and Spanish civilians were such authors as Finestres, Sala, Murillo …*"[71]

---

70. O.F. Robinson, T.D. Fergus, W.M. Gordon, *European Legal History*, Butterworths, 1996, 2nd ed., p.118–119.

71. See *Continental Legal History* supra note 69 at p.579–683.

"*Spain ... reacted to French domination under Napoléon by wishing to break immediately with the French code, while nevertheless recognizing the advantages of codification. The Spanish legal tradition however was not uniform ... Throughout the nineteenth and twentieth centuries, the political history of Spain had been fraught as the result of a continual tension between liberalist and absolutist forces ... Several codifications were made in Spain during the nineteenth century with successive criminal codes in 1810, 1822 ... and commercial codes in 1829 and 1885. It was 1889 however before a civil code was introduced, and it bore the imprint not only of the French but also Italian influence.*"[72]

---

72. See Watkin supra note 48 at p.144.

Chapter 2

Codification

A. Codification in France and Louisiana

1. Codification in France

"The driving force behind the movement for codification (the term itself, like many other in the legal literature of the age, was an invention of Jeremy Bentham) was a highly urgent desire for legal unity. The revolutionary age needed a speedy means of bringing about the centralization of judicial administration, which it discovered in codification ... The reception of Roman law had provided a basic law for most of Continental Europe, but this European 'common' law had only subsidiary force in the absence of provincial, territorial, or town law ... The urge was particularly great to unify and reduce the civil law to writing, for upon the civil law depended the expansion of trade and commerce which was taking place on the eve of the French Revolution. The first and primary concern of the movement for codification being the civil law, codification has traditionally remained synonymous with civil codification.... The idea of codification appealed mightily to the French philosophers. 'Let all laws be clear, uniform, and precise,' said Voltaire. 'If laws are simple and clear,' said the Abbé de Mably, 'there is no need for much study to make a good judge.' But they only repeated with perhaps a more popular accent what had become an article of faith of the school of natural law. Legislation was simply human reason made concrete in a particular set of circumstances ... [S]ince the law of nature was not only discoverable but immutable, it could be reduced to a permanent body of rules, known and accessible to all and sundry, and would never be in need of change ... The Roman law might express many of the principles of natural law, but these needed to be universalized to meet the requirements

43

of the new age. If in fact the systems of natural law were not always precisely alike, there was all the more reason for authoritative settlement by means of a code ..."[73]

As seen above, at the time of the French Revolution of 1789, the country was divided into some 65 general customs and 300 local ones in the northern part of the kingdom. The south was under the influence of the written Roman law under the form of the Barbarian compilations. The Revolution severed the past from the future with the codification of several fields of law as a result of Napoleon's decisive intervention.[74] The French Constitution of 1791 stated in its first title that "[t]here shall be made a code of all the civil laws common to the realm." However, the Constituent Assembly undertook, first to write a criminal code, which was adopted in 1791. As far as the private law was concerned, the Constituent Assembly had some difficulty tackling some legal institutions like marriage, divorce, successions and property. It will be under the governance of another assembly, the Convention, that drafts of civil codes will be undertaken. In the month of August 1793, **Cambacérès**, then president of the committee on legislation, presented a first draft of a civil code to the Convention. It had taken two months for Cambacérès and his committee to put together this draft of 719 articles following the plan of Justinian's Institutes (persons, things, obligations, actions). This draft borrowed substantially from **Pothier** and **Guyot**.[75] The political situation, among other reasons,[76] prevented a full discussion of Cambacérès' first draft. In 1794 Cambacérès presented a second draft of a code with only 297 articles. The Convention had barely discussed the first ten articles when it decided to put it aside, as a new political turmoil was brewing.

The Convention dissolved in 1795 without having adopted a civil code. In 1796, the same Cambacérès presented a third draft of a code to another Assembly, the Council of Five Hundred, under the Directory. This third draft was 1104 articles long; it borrowed heavily from Roman law, from pre-Revolutionary French law and from Pothier. Some controversies arose on the matters of divorce, filiation (natural filiation!) and successions; this led to the failure, once again, of Cambacérès' attempts at drafting a civil code. In 1799, Jacqueminot's project did not fare better. It was then that Bonaparte came onto

---

73. William Seagle, "The Age of Codification," Chapter XVIII, *The History of Law*, Tudor Publishing, 1946, p.277–280.

74. Somewhat like Justinian in the 6th century.

75. *àuvres de Pothier, Traité des Obligations,* first published in 1761 in 2 volumes, Dabo Jeune, Libraire, Paris 1825; Guyot, see *Répertoire Universel et Raisonné de Jurisprudence Civile* (1728–1816), Pankoucke, 1779.

76. Such as, for example, the legal regime of the family which did not satisfy Napoléon Bonaparte.

the scene as the First Consul. Taking advantage of a rather stable political situation, both within and outside France, Bonaparte will put together all the component parts necessary to give France its first civil code.

Bonaparte's most skilled decision, on August 13, 1800, had been to select only a few, four, and most qualified commissioners to fulfill his goal of a civil code for France. The commissioners were: **Tronchet** [President of the Tribunal of Cassation], President of the commission, representing the customs of Paris and Orléans; a second commissioner was **Portalis**, a lawyer of great notoriety in Aix-en-Provence and a champion of Roman law; he will be selected by his peers to write the Preliminary Discourse presenting the Civil Code to the French Assemblies. Portalis has been referred to as the "Father of the Civil Code." A third commissioner was **Maleville**, a devout Catholic determined to defend religious principles. Maleville, an "avocat" (lawyer) at the Parliament of Bordeaux, represented the customs of the southwest of France and Roman law. The fourth commissioner, **Bigot de Préameneu**, a lawyer at the Parliament of Rennes and a judge at the Tribunal of First Instance in Paris, was a representative of the customs of western France.

As regards the "sources of law" that these commissioners used and incorporated in the Civil Code, there were five types: *first*, and foremost, the *written Roman law* as it was laid down in the works Pothier, the great jurist of the 18th century. Much of Pothier's writings on obligations, successions *ab intestat* and ownership will find their way into the Civil Code. A *second* major source of law for the drafters of the French Civil Code was *canon law*, particularly in the field of marriage. In addition, *customary law*, written down since Montils-les-Tours, much influenced the relationships between spouses, the community property regime, paternal authority, some forms of servitudes and rules of successions. *Another source of law* for the commissioners were the *King's ordinances* on the civil status, donations and testaments, and proof. *Lastly, the law of the Revolution*, also known as *intermediary law* had some impact on the law of marriage, hypothecs (mortgages), divorce and successions. In addition, the four commissioners used the writings of prominent jurists (doctrine) such as **Pothier, Domat, Grotius, Pufendorf, Wolff** and **Bourjon**.

Four months after having been appointed, the commissioners had completed their work: the "Projet" of the Civil Code was ready. The Projet was presented to the Tribunal de Cassation, which suggested some additions, such as the institution of "adoption," which had been turned down by the commissioners, as well as some modifications to "divorce by mutual consent." The Projet was then sent to the Courts of Appeal which made some additional observations and, subsequently, it was sent to the Council of State (Conseil d'Etat). Following many debates in that Council, its members (Cambacérès, among them) endorsed some of the recommendations made previously by the Tribunal de Cassation and the Courts of Appeal, such as the institutions of "divorce by mutual consent" and "adoption" (at the urging of the First Consul Bonaparte himself!). However, the same Council deleted the Preliminary Title of 39 articles which had been written by Portalis and which included many principles of natural law based on **Domat's** Treatise on the "*Civil Laws in their Natural Order.*"[77]

After having gone through the hands of the Council of State, the Projet was communicated to the Tribunat, where it was met with a lot of hostility. The Projet of the Civil Code was threatened to fail before the Tribunat; Bonaparte reshuffled the whole make-up of this assembly, cutting it in half, so that, eventually, the Tribunat added his endorsement to the Projet. The ultimate vote on the Projet took place before the Corps Législatif on a "yes" or "no" basis. Eventually, 36 separate statutes (on 36 separate Titles) were passed in 1803–1804. After, at last, the Senate had given its approval, the First Consul "promulgated" the 36 statutes gathered together in one single code. The date was March 21, 1804 (30 ventôse year XII), and the Code was named, "**Code Civil des Français.**" It will be officially re-baptized "**Code Napoléon**" by a decree of September 3, 1807.[78]

2. Codification in Louisiana

In 1682, the French explorer Rene-Robert Cavelier Sieur de La Salle claimed the territory to the east and west of the Mississippi River for the French crown and named it "Louisiane" in honor of King Louis XIV. On September 14, 1712, a royal edict granted to Antoine Crozat, a wealthy merchant, commercial and economic control over the colony. The royal edict also provided that the legal system of Louisiana would be the *Custom of Paris*. A Superior Council was entrusted with the administration of this *Custom*; thus creating the first legal system of the territory. Both civil and criminal matters were governed by the ordinances of the kingdom. The rules of procedure in use were those of the *Châtelet* in Paris. On November 1762, by virtue of the Treaty of Fontainebleau, the King of France ceded the Louisiana territory to his cousin, the King of Spain. This first treaty was confirmed by the Treaty of Paris on February 10, 1763. After the first Spanish governor was evicted by the French colonists, a new gov-

---

77. It is important to add that the First Consul himself attended and presided over 55 of the 106 meetings of the commission.

78. Jean-Louis Halpérin, *L'Histoire de la fabrication du code. Le code: Napoléon?*, in *Le Code civil*, No. 107, Seuil, 2003.

ernor, Alejandro O'Reilly, took firm control of the territory and quelled the re-
bellion in October 1768. On November 25, 1769, O'Reilly introduced a major
change in the then French legal system implemented in the territory. O'Reilly
announced, in a "proclamation," that an "abstract" of the Spanish laws understandable by all would now become the law of the land. As a consequence, the
French inhabitants had to become familiar with Spanish law and the Spanish
language, to find out that, after all there were no fundamental differences, or
at least no such differences as to justify their original fear at the change of governmental rulers and legal system. By the Treaties of San Ildefonso and Madrid,
1800–1801, Spain returned the territory of Louisiana to France. In the month
of May 1803, the "Louisiana Purchase," under the form of the Treaty of Paris,
was signed between the United States and France, making the territory of
Louisiana a huge part of the United States. In a ceremony on November 30,
Louisiana was officially transferred from Spain to France. On December 20,
1803, the same Louisiana was then transferred to the United States. Louisiana
became a state of the United States in 1812.

In the Act of Congress of March 26, 1804, it was stated, in Section 11, that
*"The laws in force in the said territory, at the commencement of this act ... shall
continue in force, until altered, modified, or repealed by the legislature."* A year
later, the Act of Congress of March 2, 1805, stated again, in *"Section 4 ... That
the laws in force in the said territory at the commencement of this act ... shall
continue in force, until altered, modified or repealed by the legislature."*

What did the U.S. Congress mean by *"the laws in force in the said territory ..."*? In May 1806, the "Territory of Orleans Legislative Council" adopted
an "Act" which stated:

> *"Sect. 1st. Be it therefore declared by the Legislative Council and the
> House of Representatives of the Territory of Orleans ... that the laws
> which remain in force ... are the laws and authorities following, to wit:
> 1. The Roman Civil Code, as being the foundation of the Spanish law,
> by which this country was governed before its cession to France and to
> the United States, which is composed of the institutes, digest and code of
> the emperor Justinian, aided by the authority of the commentators of the
> civil law, and particularly of Domat in his treatise of the Civil laws; ....
> 2. The Spanish law, consisting of the books of the recopilation de Castilla
> and autos accordados ...; the seven parts or partidas of the king Don
> Alphonso the learned ...; the recopilation de indias ... the laws de Toro ..."*

On June 7, 1806, the Legislative Council and the House of Representative of
the territory of Orleans passed a resolution appointing *"**James Brown and***

Moreau Lislet, lawyers, whose duty it shall be to compile and prepare, jointly, a civil code for the use of this territory. Resolved, that the two jurisconsults shall make the civil law by which this territory is now governed, the ground work of said code ..." An "Act of March 31, 1808," provided *"for the Promulgation of the Digest of the Civil Laws Now in Force in the Territory of Orleans."* In Section 1, it is stated *"That the work entitled 'Digest of the Civil Laws now in force in the territory of Orleans, with alterations and amendments adapted to its present system of government, which work is divided into three books ...' is hereby declared and proclaimed to be in force in this territory ..."* It is important to stress that the Code or Digest of 1808 was written in French after which an English translation was added.

Following a series of court rulings calling into question the authenticity and binding force of the "Digest," the Louisiana Legislature appointed a committee of three, **Edward Livingston**, **Louis Moreau Lislet** and **Pierre Derbigny**, to remodel the Code of 1808 *"in such manner as they shall deem advisable."* By the Act of April 12, 1824 the *"Code"* prepared by the three commissioners was adopted and promulgated on May 20, 1825. Again, this *"Code"* of 1825 was written in French with a translation in English subsequently added to it. The purpose of this Code of 1825 was mostly to consolidate the civil laws then in existence and to eradicate the uncertainties caused by the courts, which had not been given much guidance on the interpretation of the Digest of 1808.

As a result of the Civil War and constitutional changes which culminated in the Reconstruction Constitution of Louisiana of 1868, a new revision of the Civil Code became a necessity. In 1869 a joint legislative committee was charged with revising and updating the Code of 1825. The new Civil Code was promulgated in March 1870. This Code of 1870 was written in English and no translation in any language was made.[79]

B. Codification[80]

1. Codification: Concept and Misconceptions

As seen above, the Code of Hammurabi, the Twelve Tables, the Corpus Juris Civilis, the French Civil Code and the Louisiana Civil Code were the products

---

79. On the history of Louisiana law and the Codes of 1808 and 1825, see *Moreau Lislet: The Man Behind the Digest of 1808*, Alain Levasseur and Vincent Feliú, Claitor's Publishing Division, 2008.

80. See *Dictionary of the Civil Code*, LexisNexis, 2014; word: codification: "the process of putting together a code and the outcome of the process."

of a combination of phenomena, which had in common at least three kinds of original identifying features. There were some *social features*, which manifested themselves in pitting different classes of society against each other. There were, for instance, eras when the weak but numerous were rising against the few but powerful, or the rich against the poor or, still, the educated against the illiterate. There were also, obviously, *political features* involved, such as an extensive reach of power and control on the part of kings, emperors, political and often military leaders. There were also instances of assertion of political independence from other sovereigns as well as harsh manifestations of sovereignty over territories and their people combined, at times, with the belief of acting for the good of the people. In the end, such works, whether compilations, codicis, or codes, could not have been undertaken and completed without the involvement of men learned in the law, the true technicians, engineers, skilled in drafting and expressing the law in some "codified" form. They were, early on, the Praetors and the jurists of the classical period of Rome, the professors and jurists of Justinian, followed by the judges, the professors and the avocats of Bonaparte. Only they, acting and working together as men learned in the law, could assemble masses of texts of different origins and, often, of different forms; only they could identify and select the texts that should be preserved, as they felt that those texts were destined to last into a glorious future. Only they could be charged with writing down the law in simple, clear, understandable and broad dispositions or articles. As a product of centuries of learning, discussing, arguing, writing, the *jus civile* culminated in the creation of the most widely spread legal tradition in our days: the civil law tradition and its expression in the form of "civil codes."

In the civil law tradition, one common trait of the great majority of the civil law systems in existence today is that they have **codes** of law and, in particular, **civil codes**.

In the newly available *Dictionary of the Civil Code*[81] a **code** is described, in a <u>formal sense</u>, as a *"collection of laws; more precisely, official collection of legislative and regulatory provisions governing a specific field (ex. Penal Code, IP Code) often with an indication of the country of origin (ex. Italian Civil Code, Swiss Code of Obligations); refers to the aggregate of texts, directly from the source, which are combined in the original and only official edition; thereafter they are combined in private editions (in conformity with the original edition but completed with the incorporation of subsequent legislation); by extension, the publication support, the actual volume."*

---

81. See *Dictionary of the Civil Code*, LexisNexis, 2014.

The same dictionary describes a **code** in a <u>scientific sense</u> as a *"consistent body of rules governing a specific field; body of legal rules in a given field, stemming from the compilation and arrangement of rules relating to it (usually according to a systematic organization); however, it may turn out to be a codification in the true sense (codification that may change the law) or a purely formal and clerical codification (consolidation of existing law)."* In this respect, the French Civil Code of 1804 and the Louisiana Civil Code of 1808 were more illustrations of a *"codification in the true sense"* rather than a codification in a *"formal and clerical sense,"* since they did indeed bring about major changes in the laws and legal systems of France and Louisiana.

A **code**, as a form of expression of rules of law, is the product of *"[t]he process of putting together a code and the outcome of the process."*[82] An understanding of the concept of codification is described in the same dictionary as *"[d]rawing up a code arising from a movement of reform; codification called real (réelle) leading to a new work, meant to gather together, set, clarify, renovate, systematize, unify rules concerning a subject matter by arranging them in a new body of law that has the force of legislation; ... codification based on pre-existing sources (ex. the Civil Code of 1804, a work synthesizing the pre-revolutionary law, the intermediary law, the royal ordinances, etc. ...); revising and restructuring in the Code some entire parts, sections ...; one could refer to this form of codification as codification of a new body of law."*

Behind these legalistic and technical terms, we can hear Portalis advising the Assemblies that *"legislation is not a pure act of power; it is an act of wisdom, justice and reason. The legislator does not exercise authority as much as he serves a sacred office. He must not forget that legislation is made for men, and that men are not made for legislation; that it should be adapted to the character, habits, and position of the people for whom it is made; ... The Codes of nations are the fruit of the passage of time; but properly speaking, we do not make them."*[83]

A **civil code** was considered therefore to be a need both by the people of France and Louisiana. It had become essential to adapt the Code to their *"character, their habits and position."* Since France and Louisiana are still governed today by civil codes, it must be because a code does present some inherent beneficial features and, obviously, allows for a reasonable adaptation and implementation of the legal rules it formulates. Otherwise how could these civil codes have lived to be more than two centuries old? As Portalis stated in a few sentences that encompass the essence of the civil law system and the whole

---

82. See *Dictionary of the Civil Code*, LexisNexis, 2014; word: codification.
83. See Levasseur supra note 9 at p.767, 773.

spirit of the working relationship between the legislator, the courts and the ju-rists, *"The role of legislation is to set, by taking a broad approach, the general propositions of the law, to establish principles which will be fertile in application, and not to get down to the details of questions which may arise in particular in-stances. It is for the judge and the jurist, imbued with the general spirit of the laws, to direct their application."*[84]

In a publication from which we will purposefully quote extensively here, the Law Reform Commission of Canada meant to dispel existing myths, an-tagonisms and misconceptions about codification and the civil law tradition, on the one hand, and about the common law as well, on the other hand.[85] With respect to the "Biases Regarding Codification" we have selected the fol-lowing excerpts, which we consider extremely relevant and instructive:

a. Biases Regarding Codification

1.41. *Codified law is barren and sterile, or so we are often told. Because it is writ-ten, it is said to be too rigid, to leave insufficient room for judicial creativity, to curtail the judge's discretionary powers (which powers are seen to guarantee eq-uity and justice), and to be unresponsive to changing social reality ...*

1.42. *No great effort is required to realize that such attacks on codification are unfounded and betray a lack of understanding of what codification really is.... [P]eople now realize that adapting law to a changing society is very often more a task for the legislator than for the judge: witness the impressive development of statutory law in common law countries since the nineteenth century.*

1.43. *Some English lawyers have recognized the absurdity of such reasoning. "Not even the French codes (relatively the most rigid of all) have proved inflexible, and the German and Swiss codes ... have created systems which are far less rigid than ours...."* (Gardiner, B. and Martin A., Law Reform Now, London, 1964)

1.44. *The attitude of some people toward codification once again is based on mis-conception. To begin with, codification does not mean that the entire body of law must be set down in the finest detail ... In that sense, the notion of a 'complete' code is mythical, absurd and utopian ... [Codification's purpose] is achieved if it expresses in clear terms the general rules and the basic, distinctive principles of [criminal law ...] The Code should contain guiding principles for both judges*

---

84. *Id* at page 769. We will illustrate and give examples of this profound and meaning-ful statement in the second part of this book.

85. *Towards a Codification of Canadian Criminal Law*, Law Reform Commission of Canada, Department of Justice of Canada, Ottawa, 1976.

and lawyers ... It should reflect the positive law in a series of clear, simple rules deliberately shorn of countless details ...

1.45. *Secondly, codification must not be considered as a vote of non-confidence in the courts or as something that will suppress their creativity to the point of reducing them to "judging machines." It has been said less frequently that codification removes all elasticity from the application of the law by reducing or eliminating judicial discretion ... As paradoxical as it may seem, in practice a code leaves judges more freedom and discretion than they have under the binding authority of precedent ... Except in the United States, outright refusal to follow the precedent is very rare ... The so-called "elasticity" of the common law means only that its accumulated precedents constitute innumerable fine points ...*

1.46. *Far from eliminating judicial discretion, a code actually strengthens it in two ways. First, in a codified system the judge must continually use his discretion to interpret legislation and the concepts embodied therein ... In addition, codes contain several articles worded so as to allow the judge to adapt them to circumstances ...* [The purpose of the 2nd part of this book dealing with methods of interpretation will stress the truth of this statement, and the examples given of the methods of interpretation will further illustrate the major role judges play in interpreting code articles with the help and support of "doctrine."]

1.47. *Thirdly, codified law is as responsive to social change as common law ...* [Again, the 2nd part will provide illustration of such an assertion.]

1.48. *Finally, part of codified law consists of general principles.* [See the 2nd part of this book for illustrations.]

1.49. *Fear that a codified system may age prematurely and become outmoded is often the consequence of confusion between statute and code. In the purest British tradition, a statute should spell out everything down to the smallest detail. Its criteria of excellence are meticulousness and precision ... To judge codified law by the canons of statutory law ... is to overlook the fact that the former is based on essentially different criteria of generality, simplicity and conciseness. It is not concerned with foreseeing all circumstances and covering all the details of every conceivable case. Its only purpose is to lay down the basic principles of the law from which practical applications can then logically be derived. Being abstract and general, it is able to include all cases within its scope without explicitly solving each one, thus leaving sufficient room for a large amount of judicial creativity.*

[**Comment**: with respect to the preceding paragraphs, and particularly **1.44**, **1.45**, **1.46** and **1.49**, the reader is urged to go back over the excerpts given above of Gaius and Justinian Institutes as well as examples of articles of the Louisiana

Civil Code. They do provide instructive illustrations of the general and broad statements of principles of law included in the articles. There are no details and, therefore, they call upon the courts and doctrine for their interpretation and application. See also Part II for additional illustrations.]

2. The Process of Codification

Since Portalis was most instrumental in giving to the French Civil Code its preeminence in devising and implementing this new form of legislation, it is appropriate and legitimate to present his thoughts and his advice on the original task he and his peers had been entrusted with: to draft a civil code for the people of France.

The following few excerpts encapsulate the whole essence of what the civil law is all about. They stress two major features of the fundamental nature of the civil law. It is, first, a functional relationship between the legislator, the courts and the jurists, i.e., doctrine, as being the "creative sources of law." It is, in addition, the embodiment of an interdependence, an intertwined relationship between these three sources of law in such a way that they are destined to work closely together. These two major identifying features of the civil law find their expression in the process of codification.

a. Legislation and Codification: Where Is the Difference?

As regards the actual process of codification as distinguished from the process of legislation, Portalis instructed the Assemblies in these words:

"What a task it is to draft civil legislation for a great people! The work would exceed human strength, if it involved giving this people an absolutely new institution, and if, forgetting it occupies the highest rank among civilized nations, we chose to ignore the experience of the past and the tradition of common sense, rules, and maxims which has come down to us and embodies the spirit of centuries.

Legislation is not a pure act of power; it is an act of wisdom, justice and reason. The legislator does not exercise authority as much as he serves a sacred office. He must not forget that legislation is made for men, and that men are not made for legislation; that it should be adapted to the character, habits, and position of the people for whom it is made; … while it is possible in a new undertaking to calculate the advantages a theory offers, it is impossible to anticipate all the drawbacks that practice alone can reveal; …

At the beginning of our discussions, we could not help being surprised by the opinion so widely held that, in drafting a civil code, a few precise provisions on each subject would suffice and that the great art is to simplify everything while foreseeing everything.

To simplify everything is an undertaking on the meaning of which we would all have to agree. To anticipate everything is a goal impossible of attainment ...

[We] find in the codes of civilized nations the kind of meticulous attention which covers a multiplicity of particular issues and seems to make an art of reason itself. Thus we did not think we should simplify the laws to the point of leaving citizens without rule or guarantee concerning their greatest interests. We also kept clear of the dangerous ambition of wanting to forecast and regulate everything. No matter what we do, positive laws could never entirely replace the use of natural reason in the affairs of life ... ; the legislator cannot possibly provide for all eventualities ... There is a host of details which either escape him or are too much open to contention or instability to become the subject of a legal provision. In any case, how can one resist the course of events or the steady pressure of customs? How can one know and calculate in advance what only experience can reveal? ... A code, however complete it may seem, is hardly finished before a thousand unexpected issues come to face the judge ... A host of things is thus necessarily left to the province of custom, the discussion of learned men, and the decisions of judges ... The role of legislation is to set, by taking a broad approach, the general propositions of the law, to establish principles which will be fertile in application, and not to get down to the details of questions which may arise in particular instances. It is for the judge and the jurist, imbued with the general spirit of the laws, to direct their application."[86]

[<u>Comment</u>: Portalis clearly indicates what are the sources of law in a "code" system: 1) positive laws or statutes; 2) customs; 3) judges confronted with new issues through the decisions they have to hand down; 4) the discussions of learned men. Portalis addresses also the relationship between "legislation," the "judge," and the "jurist." The latter, "imbued with the general spirit of the laws direct" the application of the laws.]

One must keep in mind that in this process of writing the law, either in a statute form or in a code:

"[T]he language of the law of a country lives in the language of that country, and it lives on it ... The language of the law is cultural language (a bond, an asset, a benefit of the legal culture) ... The language of the law is, in a major part, a legacy of tradition."[87] *... "One does not have to make a choice between 'langue-*

---

86. See Levasseur supra note 9 at p.769 [emphasis added].

87. Gérard Cornu, *Linguistique juridique*, 3ème éd., Montchrestien, 2005, p.16–19 [author's translation].

language' (of a people/nation) and 'language-language' (of a science, a disci-pline) ... The language of the law is a specific language within the maternal lan-guage that supports it. The French 'legal-juridical' language is not in conflict with the French language; it actually puts it into play; it is its implementation. How-ever, the legal- juridical language brings into the use that it makes of the French language some specific or distinctive features of terminology and of 'phraseol-ogy.'"[88] ... *"In drafting statutes, the French tradition prefers, by natural inclina-tion or liking, the concrete style. It is also, in all its brilliance and refinement, the exemplary choice of drafting of French-speaking Switzerland. The Province of Québec is also fond of it. It is the simplest, clearest, the liveliest, the most sugges-tive, the lightest ... the most French ... It is the style of Montaigne, La Fontaine, Montesquieu. Among the jurists, Domat and Pothier are not far from it. It is, for the most part, the style of the civil Code."*[89]

"The rule of law being a disposition aiming at imposing a rule of conduct under social pressure, must meet certain fundamental qualities: unity, order, precision and clarity. It must therefore be made up of words which have a clear, precise, cer-tain meaning ... Therefore one must always translate facts into a legal language to find the legal solution applicable to a given factual situation and, conversely, the legal terminology must be adapted to the appropriate qualification (or char-acterization) of the fact patterns that the legal system must regulate ... Legal terms only translate notions that state realities ... New realities must be incorporated into preexisting notions and express themselves in known words. If it is impossi-ble, new notions must be created as well as new words. But the mischaracteriza-tion or misrepresentation of notions and words is dangerous. The growth of the legal vocabulary must be justified and well thought out; it cannot be anarchical, chaotic. As a matter of principle, it is necessary also that the vocabulary be pre-cise, i.e. that the words have a meaning sufficiently refined to be identifiable and enable one to identify that which they refer to. When there is a lack of precision, the jurists strive to discover it by means of concepts and words specifically tailored. For example, behind 'fault,' they look for lists of acts caused by some 'fault.' It does happen, though, that one may have to forgo providing a precise definition when dealing with unspecified concepts, purely qualitative, which can be better under-stood than they can be defined ... 'Good morals,' 'good father of the family,'... for-mulate legal notions but they do not have any precise meaning; their pliability is the formulation of that one of the notions they refer to and that law wants pliable so that an appropriate handling can be brought to bear in all cases, even unfore-

---

88. *Id* p.316 [author's translation].
89. *Id* p.321 [author's translation].

seeable ones.... It is for doctrine to search for the substantial content of words and to devise, if necessary, the terminology capable of translating the concepts. The natural links between law, its interpretation and its application require, in spite of the variations among the professional practitioners, a uniform legal terminology. It is imperative that all the jurists speak the same language."[90]

A civil code, as a kind of expression of the legislative will, occupies a unique place within the broad concept of legislation or statutory law. A civil code is the outward cultural manifestation and orderly expression of a social and juridical system. Indeed, it transposes into code articles, mostly under the form of principles of a juridical nature, social, philosophical, economic, and moral concepts and values. These concepts and values, once they are incorporated into the work of art of codifying, become interdependent and intertwined. Therefore, to codify it is necessary to take a broad approach, to consider things as a whole and not parceled out into individual and separate units; one must think beyond the immediate factual and legal reality which is short lived so as to project it into the future under a more neutral and, sometimes, abstract legal norm.[91]

In conclusion, to *codify* is to do a lot more than to *legislate*. To codify, as Portalis explained and as Napoléon urged his commissioners to do, is to lay down the law in such a manner as to involve the reader in the many facts of his life as a person, to capture and to channel his thinking in offering to him a range of legal solutions. It is to place him in the midst of a network of relationships of all sorts, family, personal, financial, material, and physical. In a sense, a civil code displays some of the inquisitive and stimulating moves of a chess game, in which each piece attempts to carry its message following a particular pattern to reach a specific outcome or solution. Just as in a chess game, to read a civil code is to put together an array of clues, messages, and goals that can be found in the totality of a civil code and that must be carefully combined together to reach logical legal solutions. All these operations of the mind are bound by one common thread, which is that a civil code is a single unit, skillfully crafted tightly together in such a way that all its Books, Parts, Chapters, Sections, Articles can exude, behind the words that the eye and mind can read, the spirit and soul that guided and inspired the drafters of the code. The same drafters exercised their art of codifying with the knowledge and awareness that the methods of interpretation available to the jurist and the judge

---

90. Jean-Louis Bergel, *Théorie Générale du Droit,* 5ème éd., Dalloz, 2012, p.256–262 [author's translation].

91. Marie Jose Longtin, *Le style civiliste et la loi,* in *Le droit civil, avant tout un Style?,* sous la direction de Nicholas Kasirer, Thémis, 2003, p.185–205.

would lead them to uncover that spirit and soul meant to give life to the words of the law.

[**Comment**: an important point to make here is to stress, once again, the close relationship that exists because of the very essence of a civil law system, between the legislator, the judge and the jurist. It was stressed by Portalis in his *Preliminary Discourse*, where he wrote that there a line of separation between, on the one hand, the necessarily limited domain of the legislator in enacting a code and, on the other hand, the vast and varied domain of the works of the jurists and the decisions of the courts. However, these separate domains are concerning only the constitutional division among the sources of law and not at all the working relationship between these sources. By necessity, each one of these sources of law holds a position connected to the positions held by the other two sources of law, in the same manner as the three sides of an isosceles triangle are connected to each other. In this triangle, a law or a code would stand on top of the triangle, as the primary source of law, so that the two bottom sides, courts and doctrine, as secondary sources of law, would interact in their interpretation and application of the law or of articles of code.]

b. The Language of Codification

Since legislation, under the form of statutes or codes for our purpose here, is a binding source of law, and since "one may not avail himself of ignorance of the law,"[92] the law must be written so that it can be understood by its addressees. These addressees are of two broad categories: the ordinary citizen, or primary recipient on the one hand, and on the other hand, the interpreter-learned in the law, such as the judge or the jurist as the "messengers" of the legislator. The style and drafting technique of a "statute" are different from the style and drafting technique of a code. Because of these differences, the methods of interpretation applicable to one cannot always be applicable to the other. A certain method of drafting calls for a certain method of interpretation in some instances.[93]

1. A Matter of Style

The style of drafting legislation in the civil law tradition, particularly as concerns the style of drafting articles of civil codes, is original and specific in many respects. In the words of F.H. Lawson: "*The Civil Law is undoubtedly a more*

---

92. La.Civ.C. art. 5.
93. See immediately below the excerpts from Portalis.

bookish law than the Common Law ... [T]he peoples who follow the Civil Law are peoples of the book; we common lawyers are not, however many statutes our legislators may pass from time to time ... The Civil Law is literary in the more specific sense that it attracted the attention of writers of great literary power, who set themselves to expound it intelligibly and to give it the coherent form and structure of a work of art. At a stage of development before that of codification, most of the Civil Law systems were pulled into shape by institutional writers; and I am inclined to regard the influence of these institutional writers as more important than codes."[94]

"Napoléon's code has a special importance in any consideration of elegance in law because it combined in itself two distinct notions of elegance: elegance of form and elegance of style. On the on hand, the structure produced by building up the two thousand odd sections into a single unit represented the ultimate achievement of the eighteenth-century system-designers. The logical interdependence of the parts to each other and to the whole had elegance of form. On the other hand, the terse unornamented language in which the individual rules were expressed, and the precise value given to particular phrases, represented the fruit of much study of the ideal legislative style ... All literary histories cite the letter in which Stendhal explains to Balzac that when writing the Chartreuse de Parme, he often read a few pages of the Code Civil as a means of catching the plain simple style that he felt was artistically required for that work."[95]

Indeed, the style of the civil law is identified with its original and historical understanding of what a rule of law is. It does call upon a frame of mind that thinks in terms of "synthesis" and, as a consequence, in expressing the law in a concise, weighted and measured text. Since the law, because of its very nature, should be laid down under the form of a "general norm," that norm must necessarily be stated in a concise manner so as to remain general. The details, the practical instances of its implementation, and its adaptation to factual problems are for governmental regulations, court decisions and the discussions and writings of legal scholars. *"It is for the judge and the jurist, imbued with the general spirit of the laws, to direct their application ... The role of legislation ... [is] not to get down to the details of questions which may arise in particular instances."*[96]

The style of writing that is peculiar to the civil law is also intended to subject the legal norm to being interpreted and applied by the courts and doc-

---

94. *The Thomas M.Cooley Lectures,* "A Common Lawyer Looks at the Civil Law," University of Michigan Law School, 1953.

95. Peter Stein, *Elegance in Law,* 77 The Law Quarterly Review, 1961, 242–254.

96. See Levasseur supra note 9 at p.769.

trine. The courts thus become the *legislator* for a case and the jurist is a *commentator* of the case. This takes place against the background of the legal norm involved and, most likely, other legal norms. Again, as Portalis wrote:

"A host of things is thus necessarily left to the province of custom, the discussion of learned men, and the decision of judges … Interpretation by way of doctrine consists in grasping the true sense of the laws, applying them in a discerning fashion, and supplementing them in those cases which the laws have not provided for. Without this kind of interpretation could we think of fulfilling the judge's function? There is a science for lawmakers, as there is for judges; and the former does not resemble the latter … The legislator must pay attention to case law; it can enlighten him, and he can correct it; but there must be a body of case law … One cannot dispense with case law any more than he can dispense with legislation. It is to judicial decisions that we surrender the rare and extraordinary cases incapable of fitting into a mold of rational legislation … It is for experience to gradually fill up the gaps we leave …"[97]

"The real challenge of a civil code is that of not omitting something important while, at the same time, avoiding to be bogged down in details. The whole art consists in maintaining the balance between what must be stated and what should not be said … It is in facing up to this challenge that the civilian style of drafting is revealed … The civil law style is, first, a way of understanding the rule of law. It requires a great ability at synthesizing and who says synthesis, says conciseness. It is there that, in the civil law tradition, the art of making short finds its way … The conciseness of a rule of civil law is a consequence of its nature. It is first because it is a general norm that it is expressed concisely, briefly. Between the nature of a rule and its expression, there is a link of causality. The details, the precautions, the multiple objects are as sign that the rule becomes a regulation or that it usurps the function of the court. It loses then the characteristics of rule of civil law."[98]

*"Statutory laws strictly speaking differ from regulations. It is up to statutory laws to lay down in all domains the fundamental rules and to **prescribe the essential forms. The details of execution, the provisional or accidental precautions,** the immediate or variable objects, in a word, all those things which call much more upon the supervision of the authority which administers than upon the intervention of the power which establishes or creates, are of the domain of regulations. Regulations are acts of judicial administration and statutory law are acts of sovereignty. The legislator's science consists in finding in each subject the*

---

97. *Id* at p.769–773.

98. Jacques Auger, *Le style civiliste et le droit des sûretés réelles*, in *Le droit civil, avant tout un Style?* sous la direction de Nicholas Kasirer, … Editions Thémis, 2003, p.56–57 [author's translation].

principles most favorable to the common good; the judge's science is to put these principles into effect, to diversify them, and to extend them, by means of wise and reasoned application, to private causes; to examine closely the spirit of the law when the letter kills ..."[99]

"The civil law style is thus a way of devising and stating the rule, but it is also a way of applying it, interpreting it. This second feature is also a consequence of the first. Between the breadth of the rule and the specific case, there is a distance that must be reduced so as to solve the legal issue. This is the task that belongs, in the first place, to the judge. The latter is, in a sense, to use a well-known image, the legislator for particular cases. In the civil law tradition, statutory laws and cases cannot be dissociated; cases cannot possibly exist without statutory law, no more than statutory law can be conceived as being self-sufficient. At civil law, a rule of law is devised so as to be interpreted."[100]

2. The "Legistics" of a Civil Code; Drafting Technique

As concerns the nature of the language of a legal norm, because its purpose is to communicate a legal message, that message must be expressed in such a way that the language of communication must overcome the neutrality and versatility of the language of the common man. As indicated above, many words of a civil code are borrowed from the common language and become *juridicalised* once they are incorporated in the legal message that the code conveys. The word obligation, for example, is most likely understood by the common man as meaning that one has a social or moral duty to do something. But once this same word *obligation* enters the realm of the civil code, it takes on a distinct legal meaning which, itself, can take on sub-legal meanings, depending, in particular, on the adjective which could precede it or follow it. For example, the Louisiana Civil Code does make a distinction between a *natural* obligation and a *moral* obligation, as it distinguishes between a natural obligation and a civil obligation. Another distinction is made between a *real* obligation and a *personal* obligation. Thus the common and ordinary concept of obligation becomes *juridicalised* as a result of this addition of an adjective that gives to *obligation* a legal or juridical meaning.

In qualifying some concepts, as illustrated above, the codifier is pursuing a clear and specific legal purpose. Indeed, the legal meaning attached to a concept conveyed by means of a word or a group of words triggers the applica-

---

99. Jean-Etienne-Marie Portalis, *Ecrits et Discours Juridiques et Politiques*, Presses Universitaires d'Aix-Marseille, 1988, p.32 [author's translation].

100. See Auger supra note 99 at p.55–59 [author's translation].

tion of a well-defined legal regime. This legal regime is like a road map that gives an illustrated image of the legal effects of the concept hidden in a word or group of words. A shroud of legal effects surrounds what has become a legal or juridical concept. Let us take an example: in the field of *consensual juridical acts* the mere expression *oral consent or exchange of oral promises* may lead to a *binding contract* on the basis of article 1134 of the French Civil Code[101] or article 1927 of the Louisiana Civil Code.[102] Consider also, as a legal effect, that ownership is transferred "*between the parties as soon as there is an agreement on the thing and the price is fixed ...*" and furthermore, that agreement can be merely *oral* if it bears on a *movable thing*, another legal concept itself endowed with a legal regime.[103]

There are also particular words in a civil code that only have a legal meaning. These words conveying a concept are legal by their very own nature. Consider the words, and concepts therefore, of hypothec, synallagmatic, legal portion, or oblique action.[104] Outside the law, these words have no meaning. One can say, therefore, that the legal language of the law, and, as far as we are concerned, the language of a civil code in particular, is also a technical and scientific language. There is, indeed, a science of the law, "a science for lawmakers," as Portalis wrote, just as there is a science of mathematics, chemistry, et cetera. That science of law, legal science, can be learned and taught as can the other sciences which are framed by a technical and special language as well

---

101. Fr. Civ. C. art. 1134: **Effects of Obligations**. Agreements lawfully entered into have the force of law for those who have made them. They may be revoked only by their mutual consent, or for causes authorized allowed by law. They must be performed in good faith.

102. La. Civ. C. art. 1927: **Consent**. A contract is formed by the consent of the parties established through offer and acceptance. Unless the law prescribes a certain formality for the intended contract, offer and acceptance may be made orally, in writing, or by action or inaction that under the circumstances is clearly indicative of consent.

Unless otherwise specified in the offer, there need not be conformity between the manner in which the offer is made and the manner in which the acceptance is made.

103. Fr. Civ. C. art. 1583: **The nature and form of sale**. It is perfect between the parties and the ownership is acquired as of right by the buyer with regard to the seller as soon as they have agreed on the thing and on the price, although the thing has not yet been delivered nor the price paid.

. La. Civ. C. art. 2456: **Transfer of ownership**. Ownership is transferred between the parties as soon as there is agreement on the thing and the price is fixed, even though the thing sold is not yet delivered nor the price paid.

104. Hypothec (Fr. Civ. C. art. 2393; La. Civ. C. art. 3278, mortgage); synallagmatic (Fr. Civ. C. art. 1102; La. Civ. C. art. 1908); legal portion (Fr. Civ. C. art. 745; La. Civ. C. art. 888); oblique action (Fr. Civ. C. art. 1166; La. Civ. C. art. 2044). See: Dictionary of the Civil Code.

as by a particular frame of mind and the use of technical and appropriate tools, instruments, and/or rules.

Since a civil code is the legal expression of the values, principles, beliefs and aspirations of a particular people, as was the case of the law of the Twelve Tables or the Digest of Justinian, the language of a civil code is, as we have seen, the legal language of the culture of that particular people. That country that has adopted its "Civil Code," that "Civil Code," being the written expression of a culture, lives that culture and it lives it daily. It also expresses that culture in a legal language that is itself, the cultural language of that people or that country. It is in these differences in culture that we find the explanation of the differences between the civil codes of civil law jurisdictions, such as between the Louisiana Civil Code, the French Civil Code and the Québec Civil Code, in such fields as successions and marriage for example. A civil code of a people is therefore based on the social, sociological, philosophical, economic values and aspirations of that people. These values and aspirations are then transposed into a legal language peculiar to that code.

Within a particular civil code, such as the Louisiana Civil Code, a series of useful cross-references can be made to illustrate the fact that there is an intended and necessary harmonious symbiosis in a code. Just as the "movements" in a symphony are intertwined and merged under one title, likewise the different Books, Parts, Chapters, Sections in a code have all been bound indivisibly together by the art of codification that inspired and guided the skilled hands of the codifiers. For example, the code articles on Parents and Children cannot be dissociated from the code articles on Successions, or on Matrimonial Regimes, or on Liability; the code articles on law of Sale cannot be dissociated from the code articles on Things, Obligations, Contracts, or Securities.

By its structure, its breadth, its general provisions but also, paradoxically, by its brevity, a code is necessarily and we would say intentionally meant to be flexible, malleable, bordering on vagueness at times. Just like a society is neither monolithic nor immutable, a civil code must be capable of evolving, adapting and adjusting because it must be, for a judge, the source of the law on which the judge will base his decision. As the Canadian commission clearly explained, a code is made to breathe, to live over a long period of time so that it can be matched with the life of the people for which it is a guide of conduct vis-à-vis "Persons" and "Things."[105]

---

105. La. Civ. C., Book I, *Of Persons*; Fr. Civ. C., Book I, *Des Personnes*. La. Civ. C., Book II, *Things and the Different Modifications of Ownership*; Fr. Civ. C., Book II, *Des Biens et Des Différentes Modifications de la Propriété*.

In the Section that follows immediately below and in the 2nd part of this book, we will endeavor to show, by means of illustrations, why a code is not a sterile exercise in legistics,[106] why a code is not meant to stop the movement of time. As we hope to be able to show, a civil code is meant to be and actually is a vote of confidence and trust by the legislator in the judges and the jurists who are the interpreters and, in a sense, the "enforcers" of his work: a civil code.

3. Illustrations of the "Legistics"[107] of a Civil Code; Structure of Code Articles

An important contribution of the legal language to the art of drafting code articles at civil law, consists in finding out the best way of actually structuring a sentence, assembling skillfully together a series of words so as to convey an accurate legal message under an appropriate form. That form will necessarily depend on the nature of the legal norm that is to be drafted. For example, a principle embodying a moral value, such as the principle of unjust enrichment, or a principle embodying a philosophical value, such as the principle that property is for the living, or a principle reflecting a sociological and behavioral value, such as the principle that one should help one's neighbor, cannot be phrased and written in the same manner and style as a specific legal rule on prescription (acquisitive prescription, for example), or on the form of a juridical act (a testament, for example), or on the formalities of marriage, etc. ... The phraseology of a civil code article, its legistics, its syntax, will be for the interpreter, be it a judge or a jurist, a meaningful and instructive guide or map to look into the meaning, purpose and scope of application of a code article. This is where the different methods of interpretation, some based on the words used in a code article and others based on the undisclosed, but behind the scene, "reason or reasons" that motivated the legislator to draft a code article as it did, will become creative instruments in the hands of the court or the jurist.

Let us consider the linguistic and grammatical structures of some code articles of today and compare them, where possible, with some statements from

---

106. The French word is "légistique." A translation and explanation are given in footnote 107.

107. **Légistique:** "Science of drafting statutes; more specifically the systematic study of the different methods to draft or write texts of statutes." In English: **legislative science,** *Dictionary of the Civil Code,* LexisNexis, 2014. We will be using the word "legistics" in English as the equivalent of "légistique" in French.

Gaius' Institutes of the 2nd century and Justinian's Institutes or Digest of the 6th century. Despite the many centuries that separate Gaius' and Justinian's Institutes or Digest from the 19th-century French and Louisiana Civil Codes, we will have to acknowledge the obvious, which is the existence of common features between the Institutes and the Civil Codes mentioned. These features are inherent in the process of codification and are rooted in the Roman law style or civil law style of drafting. The features of this "legistics" or drafting technique are based on a simple and, yet, fundamental binomial. It consists in presenting, first, an hypothesis under the form of a broad statement of facts; this statement of facts is followed, in second place, by a statement of the applicable law, in other words: the legal solution. It ensues, as we will explain in the second part of this book, that when "the facts" of the hypothesis broadly described in a code article and the "new facts" in a case submitted to the court or the jurist are similar so that the latter can fit in the former, then the "law," the legal solution applicable to the "new" facts, ought to be the same as the legal solution stated in the code article. On the other hand, when the "new facts" of a case before the court cannot fit under the facts of the hypothesis given in one article or two or more articles, then the judge who must rule in the case will have to go beyond the words of the code articles. In doing so, the judge, or the jurist, will ponder over the reason or reasons that inspired and motivated the legislator to enact rules of law for a variety of hypotheses which do have <u>something</u> in common with the new facts presented to the court. That <u>something</u>, the judge or the jurist will be able to discover by using methods of interpretation based, first, on <u>semantics</u> to ascertain the meaning, broad or narrow, of the words used by the legislator, and/or, in second place, on methods of interpretation based on the <u>reason or reasons</u>, the motives/intentions that justify and provide the foundation of the law.

Let us focus, here, on the "legistics" or drafting technique of some articles, their syntax and grammatical structure. We have selected examples from sources of law previously mentioned: Gaius, Justinian, the French Civil Code and the Louisiana Civil Code.

Gaius: De Rebus—Of Things[108]

 # 70. Alluvial accretions to our land become ours, again by natural law. That is held to be an accretion by alluvion which a river adds to our land so gradually that it is impossible to estimate how much is being added at any particular mo-

---

108. See Zulueta supra note 28 at p.83.

ment; whence the common saying, that an addition is by alluvion if it is so grad-
ual as to be invisible.

Comment: "Alluvial accretions to our land" is the "hypothesis," a fact that
occurs naturally; the "law" applicable to this fact is: "becomes ours, again by
natural law." Then follows a definition of accretion so as to help the Praetor
and the Judex in being able to identify an alluvial accretion and provide a legal
solution.

#71. Accordingly, if a river tears away a piece of your land and carries it down to
mine, that piece remains yours.

Comment: the facts are described in the words: "if a river tears away a piece
of your land and carries it down to mine," and the law is "that piece remains
yours."

 # 73. Furthermore, what a man builds on my land becomes mine by natural
law, although he built on his own account, because a superstructure goes with
the land.

Comment: we find the facts in the following: "what a man builds on my
land.... Although he built on his account ..." and the law is: "becomes mine
by natural law ... because a superstructure goes with the land."

Justinian: Lib. II.Tit. I. De Rerum Divisione[109]

#29. If a man builds upon his own ground with the materials of another, he is con-
sidered the proprietor of the building, because everything built on the soil accedes to
it. The owner of the materials does not, however, cease to be owner, only while the
building stands he cannot claim the materials, or demand to have them exhibited ...

Comment: the facts are stated in the following: "If a man builds upon his
own ground with the materials of another." The law then is: "he is considered
the proprietor of the building, because everything built on the soil accedes to
it." An additional legal rule follows: "The owner of the materials ... exhibited ..."
This additional legal rule then finds an application in this last sentence below.

#29: ... But if the building is destroyed from any cause, then the owner of the ma-
terials, if he has not already obtained the double value, may reclaim the materi-
als, and demand to have them exhibited.

Comment: a first set of facts or an element of the hypothesis is given in the
very first statement, as explained in the comment immediately above. This

---

109. Thomas Sandars, *The Institutes of Justinian*, 2nd ed., Gaunt Inc., 1997.

statement goes on to say: "but if the building is destroyed from any cause ... (and) if he has not already obtained the double value." The law applicable then becomes that "the owner of the materials ... may reclaim the materials, and may demand to have them exhibited."

Justinian: Lib. IV.Tit. Ill. De lege Aquilia

 # 3. Nor is a person made liable by this law, who has killed by accident, provided there is no fault on his part, for this law punishes fault as well as willful wrong-doing.

Comment: the facts are stated in very few words: "who has killed by accident" and the law then becomes, "[n]or is a person made liable by this law ... provided there is no fault on his part, for this law punishes fault as well as willful wrong-doing."

 # 6. So again, a physician who has performed an operation on your slave, and then neglected to attend to his cure, so that the slave dies, is guilty of a fault.

Comment: the facts make up most of the statement: "So again, a physician who has performed an operation on your slave, and then neglected to attend to his cure, so that the slave dies." The law then becomes, "is guilty of a fault."

French Civil Code[110]

Article 555 #1: *When plantings, constructions, or works have been made by a third person and with materials belonging to him, the owner of the premises has the right, subject to the provisions of paragraph 4, either to keep the ownership of them, or to compel the third person to remove them.*

Comment: the facts, the hypothesis, is in that part of the sentence starting with: "When plantings ..." and finishing with: "belonging to him." The law is then stated starting with: "the owner of the premises...." and finishing with: "to remove them."

Article 556. *Deposits of earth and accretions that gather successively and imperceptibly on riparian lands are called alluvion.*

Alluvion benefits the riparian owner, whether it is a domanial stream or not; on the condition, in the first case, that he leaves a footpath or tow-path, in accordance with regulations.

---

110. English translation for Legifrance 2013. Translation by Alain Levasseur (LSU), Randall Trahan (LSU) and David Gruning (LOYOLA).

Comment: as we had in Gaius #70, this article gives a definition of alluvion or a statement of the facts in the first paragraph. In the second paragraph, the law is given first: "alluvion benefits the riparian owner" and, to the facts given in the first paragraph, additional facts are here given regarding "whether it is a stream, domanial or not."

Article 1382. *Every act whatever of man that causes damage to another, obliges him by whose fault it occurred to repair it.*

Comment: the whole law of civil liability in French law is summarized in this broad and concise statement, the origin of which can be found in the Lex Aquilia of the Romans (see supra Justinian). Notice how broadly the facts or hypothesis are stated: "Every act whatever of man that causes damage to another." Every single word in this hypothesis lends itself to a very broad interpretation. We shall see in the next part of this book how this article has been interpreted over the decades of its existence. The law in this same Article 1382 is briefly stated as follows: "obliges him by whose fault it occurred to repair it."

Louisiana Civil Code

Article 499 #1. *Accretion formed successively and imperceptibly on the bank of a river or stream, whether navigable or not, is called alluvion. The alluvion belongs to the owner of the bank, who is bound to leave public that portion of the bank which is required for the public use.*

Comment: as was the case of #70 of Gaius' Institutes and of Article 556 of the French Civil Code, this Article 499 paragraph 1 of the Louisiana Civil Code starts with a definition of "alluvion." This definition is also combined with a statement of facts: "Accretion formed successively and imperceptibly on the bank of a river or stream, whether navigable or not, is called alluvion." The legal solution is to the effect that "the alluvion belongs to the owner of the bank ..."

Article 2315 A. *Every act whatever of man that causes damage to another obliges him by whose fault it happened to repair it.*

Comment: considering the exact similarity of this Article of the Louisiana Civil Code with Article 1382 of the French Civil Code, the exact same comment made under Article 1382 of the French Civil Code can be transposed here.

Article 86. *Marriage is a legal relationship between a man and a woman that is created by civil contract ...*

Comment: the facts are briefly stated as "a man and a woman," and the law is stated as a man and a woman entering into a "marriage [which] is a legal relationship ... created by civil contract."

Sometimes the hypothesis or fact pattern necessary to a rule of law is in an article other than the article in which a rule of law is stated. For example, the hypothesis for Louisiana Civil Code Article 1879 is stated much earlier in Article 1756.

Article 1756. *An obligation is a legal relationship whereby a person, called the obligor, is bound to render a performance in favor of another, called the obligee. Performance may consist of giving, doing, or not doing something.*

Article 1879. *Novation is the extinguishment of an existing obligation by the substitution of a new one.*

Comment: in other words, binding obligations must exist (<u>as a fact</u>) before novation (<u>as a legal effect</u>) can take place.

[*Observation*: from the examples given above of written sources of civil law across different centuries, we can draw the conclusion that there exists a legislative technique of drafting a civil law norm, a "legistics" particular to a "civil code," and that this technique is actually an "art" consisting in "simplifying everything while foreseeing everything."[111] Once the legislator has fulfilled its role in taking a broad approach, in setting some general propositions of the law, then "it is for the judge and the jurist, imbued with the general spirit of the laws, to direct their application."[112]

---

111. See Levasseur supra note 9 at p.768.
112. See Levasseur supra note 9 at p.769.

Part II

Interpretation and Reasoning

Our purpose in the second part of this book is not at all to engage in a the-oretical debate on the merits or drawbacks of the interpretation process of a civil code as opposed to the interpretation process of statutes. Rather, we do intend to focus on the interpretation of statutes and civil codes from a practi-cal point of view. We hope that this practical approach will serve the reader, versed or not in legal matters, understand and appreciate the role that courts and doctrinal writers play in applying and interpreting any form of positive law, be it a statute or a civil code. Before embarking on this practical perspec-tive of the process of interpretation, we will endeavor to offer a kind of road map or guide on how to "read" a statute, in general, by focusing our attention on the statutory provisions of a civil code with specific references to the Louisiana Civil Code. Thereby, we will strive to help the reader understand what is taking place through the process of interpretation by describing the ex-isting methods of interpretation and their implementation by means of a va-riety of techniques of interpretation. In a second part, we will illustrate the outcomes, or results, of these techniques as we apply them to some articles of the Louisiana Civil Code. Then we will *dissect* some decisions of the Louisiana Supreme Court by pointing out the techniques of interpretation the Court re-sorted to in some instances in reaching their decisions, as well as pointing out the techniques, or means of interpretation, that could be used to reach a dif-ferent, and sometimes opposite, result.

Chapter 1

Interpretation: Process and Methods

Since this book might be read (and, hopefully used) by jurists and lawyers trained in the common law who might be interested in finding out how a "civilian" can possibly make sense of civil code articles that give so little guidance to the court, we will first begin by providing the views of a few "common law scholars" and "civil law scholars" on the meaning and understanding of the notion of "interpretation of statutes." We will examine this notion in general while also focusing on the purpose that is to be achieved by this intellectual process of interpreting statutes. In the second section we will present the views of some civil law scholars on the "interpretation of a civil code" as a special kind of statute.

A. Interpretation of Statutes: Common Law and Civil Law Perspectives

1. Common Law Perspective

In the second edition of *Statutes and Statutory Construction* by J.G. Sutherland and John Lewis (1904), we are told that "*Dr. Lieber defines interpretation as 'the art of finding out the true sense of any form of words; that is, the sense which their author intended to convey, and of enabling others to derive from them the same idea which the author intended to convey.' He uses this word in a sense distinct from construction. [He says: 'Construction is the drawing of conclusions respecting subjects that lie beyond the direct expression of the text, from elements known from and given in the text. Conclusions which are in the spirit though not in the letter of the text.' Hermeneutics, 44]. These words, however, are generally used interchangeably and as practically synonymous. The literal interpretation of a statute is finding out its true sense according to Dr. Lieber's definition—by making the statute its own expositor. If the true sense can thus be discovered, there is no resort to construction. The certainty of the law is next in importance to its justice. And if the legislature has expressed its intention in the law itself, with certainty, it is not admissible to depart from that intention on any extraneous consideration or theory of interpretation."*[113] Professor Singer added: *"This distinction is not helpful. It is generated by the obsolete idea that words 'mean' something in themselves ... Theoretically, characterizing the process of decision as one of 'construction' rather than interpretation, may tend to concentrate greater attention on textual considerations. In practice, however, judicial behavior in resolving statutory issues does not appear to differ according to whether it is characterized as construction or interpretation. In this work, the terms 'interpretation' and 'construction' are used interchangeably."*[114]

In Black's Law Dictionary (Tenth Edition, 2014) under "construction," we find the following citation: *"Some authors have attempted to introduce a distinction between 'interpretation' and 'construction.' Etymologically there is, perhaps, such a distinction; but it has not been accepted by the profession. For practical purposes any such distinction may be ignored, in view of the real object of both interpretation and construction, which is merely to ascertain the meaning and will of the lawmaking body, in order that it may be enforced."*[115]

For Justice Antonin Scalia, *"What are we looking for when we construe a statute? You will find it frequently said in judicial opinions of my court and others that the judge's objective in interpreting a statute is to give effect to 'the intent of the legislature.' This principle, in one form or another, goes back to Blackstone.*[116] *Unfortunately, it does not square with some of the (few) generally accepted concrete rules of statutory construction. One is the rule that when the text of a statute is clear, that is the end of the matter. Why should that be so, if what the legislature intended, rather than what is said, is the object of our inquiry? In selecting*

---

113. J.G. Sutherland, *Statutes and Statutory Construction*, Vol. II., Chicago, 1904, p.697–698. Interpretation and construction compared.

114. Norman J. Singer, *Statutes and Statutory Construction*, 1984 Revision, p.19 § 45.04. Interpretation and construction.

115. *Black's Law Dictionary*, 10th ed., 2014; "construction," citing William M. Lile et al., *Brief Making and the Use of Law Books 337* (Roger W. Cooley & Charles Lesley Ames eds., 3d ed. 1914).

116. William Blackstone, *Commentaries on the Laws of England*, p.59–62, 91 (photo. reprint 1979) (1765).

the words of the statute, the legislature might have misspoken. Why not permit that to be demonstrated from the floor debates? […] In reality, […], if one accepts the principle that the object of judicial interpretation is to determine the intent of the legislature, being bound by genuine but unexpressed legislative intent rather than the law is only the theoretical threat. The practical threat is that, under the guise or even the self-delusion of pursuing unexpressed legislative intents, common law judges will in fact pursue their own objectives and desires, extending their lawmaking proclivities from the common law to the statutory field.... As Dean Landis of Harvard Law School (a believer in the search for legislative intent) put it in a 1930 article: 'The gravest sins are perpetrated in the name of the intent of the legislature. Judges are rarely willing to admit their role as actual lawgivers, and such admissions as are wrung from their unwilling lips lie in the field of common and not statute law.' "[117]

In "Statutory Interpretation," Professor Ruth Sullivan wrote, *"When judges […] interpret legislation, they purport to discover its meaning by reading the language of the text in light of the rules of statutory interpretation. This standard description of the interpretive task is misleading in a number of respects. First, the term 'discover' implies that interpreters are archaeologists rather than artists that their goal is to locate meanings fixed in the past rather than create new meanings. This may be so in theory, but in practice interpretation involves both archaeology and art. Interpreters must work with a text whose wording was fixed in the past, but in reconstructing its meaning they must draw on current knowledge and their own understanding, experience, and skills. The term 'meaning' is also misleading in so far as it brings to mind thesaura, dictionaries, and abstract definitions. What interests interpreters is not the abstract meaning of text, but its meaning in relation to particular facts. Dictionary definitions are useful as a starting point, but lawyers and judges need to know how the legislation applies to the problem with which they are dealing. It is this concrete sense of meaning—the text as it applies to particular facts—that is sought in statutory interpretation.*

Finally, the notion that statutory interpretation is a rule-governed activity is misleading. The 'rules' are not really rules, and in any event they do not really govern. At most they tell judges what should be considered in applying a text to facts. They also influence the form and content of legal argument and the rhetoric of judicial decisions. In the final analysis, however, they do not determine outcomes. The complex and subtle process by which outcomes are determined, and

---

117. *A Matter of Interpretation, An Essay by Antonin Scalia*, Princeton Univ. Press, 1997, p.16–18.

the role played by rules of interpretation in this process, are not easily pinned down. Moreover, they vary among interpreters and from one interpretative exercise to another.

... However, two things are clear. First, texts are always interpreted in relation to particular facts in light of considerations deemed relevant by the interpreter. What is deemed relevant depends on the interpreter's understanding of statutory interpretation rules. Second, while the language of the text is always important in interpretation and sometimes plays a determinative role, it is never the only relevant thing. It is impossible to fully insulate a text from its context; it is impossible to clearly distinguish among drafter, text, and interpreter."[118]

2. Civil Law Perspective

The work of reference on the interpretation of statutes and the methods of interpretation is the magnum opus of François Gény, "Méthode d'Interprétation et Sources en Droit Privé Positif" translated by the Louisiana State Law Institute as "Gény Method of Interpretation and Sources of Private Positive Law."[119]

We have selected the following excerpts among many that were just as instructive and relevant.

"Law, even in its positive form, appears to be a complex of rules which originate in the nature of things and should be derived through a more or less free interpretation from social elements which they have the purpose of ordering toward the common benefit. Law is inspired by justice and social usefulness; hence its essence places it above the formal sources which are its empirical revelations designated to direct human judgment more precisely, but which in themselves are always incomplete and imperfect.[120] ... Our principal attention with respect to statute as source of positive law ... has to be centered on the search for procedures which make it possible to derive from the statutory text the totality of rules of law it contains, with the view to their adaptation, as perfect as possible, to the circumstances of the social life. Since all rules of law in the form of statute can be considered as proposition which subordinates certain facts to an inevitable consequence, and which constitutes the major premise in a syllogism the judge will complete according to the concrete case presented to him, it becomes ultimately

---

118. Ruth Sullivan, Statutory Interpretation, p.25–26, 1997.

119. Work of Gény completed in 1899; revised and enlarged 2nd edition in 1919; reprinted in 1954; translated in 1963 by La. St. Law Inst., with Introduction by Jaro Mayda.

120. *Id.* at p.451 #183.

necessary to determine by what means will the interpreter, the necessary inter-
mediary between the legal formula and the legal practice, who prepares the way
for the task of the judge, be able to discover and adapt to concrete life both the
conditions implied in the text and the solution which it attaches to them. For this
is the proper object of legal interpretation from the practical point of view[121] *...*
[T]o interpret a statute is simply to look for the content of the legislative will with
the help of the formula in which it is expressed. As long as one stays in the sphere
of statutory interpretation proper, this search should be made without precon-
ceived ideas, about the more or less ideal form of the rule to be discovered, or about
its more or less complete adaptation to the social environment within which it is
to be applied. Of course I do not mean to say that the interpreter should elimi-
nate these considerations from his horizon. But I insist that in this situation he
can use them only to clarify his diagnosis of the legislative intent, not to dominate
and correct it ... The interpretation of a legislative text strongly resembles the in-
terpretation of a private legal document, especially a formal notarized act the con-
tent of which is expressed in an authentic formula which clearly outlines its
contours. As the private will is the soul of the legal document it created, so the leg-
islative intent alone should animate the statutory formula in which it is expressed.
This intention can be the only essential target of any statutory interpretation in
the proper sense ... [T]he statute is merely one of many elements of interpreta-
tion of law considered as a whole. Being in itself insufficient to satisfy all the needs
of human relations, which should be legally protected, it admits also other formal
sources of positive law; and in case of their default, there is still place left for free
objective search for rules. Thus, by limiting the scope of statutory rules through
strict interpretation, I end up with opening the way for other more flexible sources,
or reserving more questions for an interpretation governed simply by the princi-
ple of any scientifically objective research[122] *... Interpretation of written law would*
be in fact reduced to a too narrow field of application, with consequent meager
results, if it were to limit itself exclusively to the formulation of the text and not
step out of the limits of its strictly intrinsic elements. Indeed, it is almost impos-
sible in practice to enclose statutory interpretation within these narrow limits ...
[A] statute is not only an intellectual phenomenon; also, and inseparably, it is a
social phenomenon, or better said, its intellectual substance is enveloped by the
social climate which determines its precise contours. Hence it is necessary to an-
alyze also this vital environment of the law or, in other words, to take into account
certain elements extraneous to the text under interpretation but in an intimate

---

121. *Id.* at p.173–174 #95.
122. *Id.* at p.181–183 #98.

contact with it, for without them the text would remain mute or would only in-
completely reveal the intent it harbors.[123] *... The problem of sources and method*
of interpretation of positive law is not resolved by means of a single key, expressed
by the often ill-understood term 'free objective search,' but implies an indivisible
group of techniques which complement each other. These techniques have been
always and perforce practiced in fact; now it is only necessary to recognize them
in law, as has been openly done in the Swiss Civil Code of 1907. They all converge
on an idea which is so evident as to be almost naïve: that law is so infinitely com-
plicated that it can not be served by simplistic formulae, but needs to evolve freely
according to its own purpose and on the basis of all available resources, as they
are implied in the various branches of human activity pursuing the 'just' and with
the different values each of them merits."[124]

Gérard Cornu and the Association Henri Capitant have defined "interprétation" in the *Vocabulaire Juridique* in its English translation as follows:
"**Interprétation:** *1. Operation or process intended to ascertain the true mean-*
ing of an obscure text; is used in reference to both the clarification given by the
act's author (interpretive law, interpretive judgment), and to the work of an in-
terpreter third party to the act (doctrinal interpretation, judicial interpretation
of contract, ministerial interpretation of a statute). 2. Word used by ext. to refer
to the method which gives rise to research (the literal interpretation focuses on
the letter of the text; the exegetic method tries to discover the intention of the
author, the teleological method is focused on the purpose of a statute)."[125]

In "Judicial Methods of Interpretation of the Law,"[126] Julio Cueto-Rua wrote:

"The judge, as a good judge, is bound to decide the case by the application of
a general rule of law which will be consistent with the meaning of the facts of the
case. That rule of law which corresponds by its meaning to the facts of the case is
the rule of law which ought to be applied. However, mere logical consistency is not
sufficient ... ; many rules may compete for application to the case, at least inso-
far as those rules in a general and direct or indirect manner describe categories of
facts under which the facts of the case may be classified. Therefore, the applica-
tion of any one of those competing rules will satisfy a basic logical prerequisite:
the facts of the case as selected and classified by the judge can be subsumed under

---

123. *Id.* at p.197 #103.
124. *Id.* at p.567–568 #224.
125. *Dictionary of the Civil Code*, LexisNexis, 2014.
126. Julio C. Cueto-Rua, *Judicial Methods of Interpretation of the Law*, Publication Institute, Paul M. Hebert Law Center, Louisiana State University, Jan. 1981.

the general normative description of antecedent facts found in the rules of law. However, neither the judge nor the parties can be indifferent to the various competing rules or to the different solutions of the conflict ... From among the competing rules of law or the competing interpretations of the same rule, he must select the rule which will lead to a just solution—a solution that will recognize the merits and demerits of the behavior of both parties and that will recognize the social interest in achieving order, security, peace, solidarity, cooperation, and justice among the members of the community. For arriving at such a just solution, the first and most important requisite is the correspondence between the meaning of the facts of the case and the meaning of the rule of law that will be applied[127] ... The proper understanding of a rule of law requires that the judge grasp its meaning, a meaning implied in the choice or preference made. To contend that the understanding of a rule of law only requires a grammatical and semantic command of the normative statement thereof implies an acute distortion of the meaning of that rule of law. This is true because such a contention ignores the axiological nature of the process by which rules of law are created—a process consisting of an evaluation of a particular social situation and the selection of certain, specific juridical consequences to be imputed to that situation on the basis of justice, solidarity, cooperation, peace, power, order and security. Furthermore, a purely historical approach is similarly narrow. A rule of law is not the end and necessary product of the development of historical forces; it is the normative expression of an act of preference taken in light of a future not yet realized. It is the future, and not so much the past, which commands the attention and interest of the legislator, for he is not a narrator of past events but the creator of new ways for the achievement of the well-being of the community.[128] ... When judges speak of the 'will' or 'intent' of the legislator, they are not referring to the actual psychological workings of each member of the legislative organ ... What the judge actually desires or requires for his task is a set of coherent and relevant data that will allow him to attribute a meaning to the rule of law, specifically a meaning which is consistent with those historical and cultural factors operative at the time the rule was enacted and which will concurrently provide a solid basis for an interpretation that is in keeping with the needs of order, security, peace, and justice, that enhances the institutions of government, and that develops social cooperation and solidarity. Therefore, the main reason behind the search for the 'will' or 'intent' of the legislator is the need to discover meanings for the rules of law under consideration which will provide an adequate normative ground for the just solution

---

127. *Id.* at p.46–47.
128. *Id.* at p.55.

of a conflict or dispute, since such a ground was not furnished by grammar or by logic alone.[129] *... It is easy to see how it is possible for the judge to bring a rule of law up to date if, instead of delving into history in an attempt to identify the elusive 'will' or 'intent' of the legislator or the objective meaning of the rule by reference to the entire historical process which led to its enactment, the judge looks to contemporary phenomena such as the people's present-day behavior, that is, the way in which the people behave under certain circumstances, and the people's spontaneous interpretation of events and their suppositions or grounds for mutual understanding. In this way, the judge could incorporate into the system both 'living law' and objective sources for the modernization of obsolete rules. Under pressing circumstances, the judge may be willing to reconsider old criteria for the interpretation of the rule of law, to set aside a meaning identified in the past, and to revise the rule in light of the new reality. The judge may validly argue that it is not so much the rule which has changed but the facts to which the rule refers. On this basis, he may work through the dialectical process of interpretation and application of the law in order to discover new meanings in old rules."*[130]

[<u>Comment</u>: in the above writings, emphasis is placed, once again, on the interconnection, the interrelationship between the legislator, the judge and the doctrinal writer as explained and illustrated in the first part of this book.]

B. Interpretation of Civil Codes

In his well known, and, dare we say, "historical" groundbreaking speech, Jean-Etienne-Marie Portalis could only make a quick reference to the methods of interpretation of the "Civil Code" he was presenting to the Assemblies on behalf of the commission. In front of such an audience, it was sufficient to describe the roles, as well as the relationships of the three parties, that would be involved in making the Civil Code, or the post-revolutionary law of the land. As regards the interpretation of the Code, Portalis stated that:

"There are two types of interpretation: one by way of doctrinal theory, and the other by way of authority ... Interpretation by way of doctrine consists in grasping the true sense of the laws, applying them in a discerning fashion, and supplementing them in those cases which the laws have not provided for. Without this kind of interpretation could we think of fulfilling the judge's function?

---

129. *Id.* at p.161–162.
130. *Id.* at p.170–171.

Interpretation by way of authority consists in resolving questions and doubts by means of regulations (règlemens) or general dispositions (dispositions générales). This last means of interpretation is the only one forbidden to the judge.

When the legislation is clear, it must be followed; when it is obscure, we must carefully analyze its provisions. If there is no particular enactment, custom or equity must be consulted. Equity is the return to natural law, when positive laws are silent, contradictory, or obscure ... The application of equity or case-by-case justice which considers and must consider, in each particular case, all the particular threads which bind one litigant to the other can never be in the legislator's domain, for he is uniquely the minister of this justice or general equity, that without regard to any particular circumstance, embraces the universality of persons and things ... Legislation governs everyone; it considers men en masse, never as individuals; it must not interfere in individual matters or lawsuits where citizens are pitted against one another.

There is a science for lawmakers, as there is for judges; and the former does not resemble the latter. The legislator's science consists in finding in each subject the principles most favorable to the common good; the judge's science is to put these principles into effect, to diversify them, and to extend them, by means of wise and reasoned application to private causes; to examine closely the spirit of the law when the letter kills ..."[131]

In the first issue of the *Revue Trimestrielle de Droit Civil*, A. Esmein wrote a provoking, for some, article entitled "Case Law and Doctrine"; he had this to say about the Civil Code and its interpretation:

"When the Civil Code, to the admiring eyes of the whole world, emerged from this long process that begins in 1789 and ends in 1804, the first task it demanded on the part of jurists consisted simply (and it was no small thing) of fixing the exact meaning of its articles and the precise scope of its provisions. It was the object of a long and painstaking application, and our schools naturally had a great part in this work. Each word was weighed, each article was examined alone and compared with those which related to the same subject. They were compared with the passages of our ancient writers, especially those of Pothier ... and, by the critical study of preparatory works an effort was made to determine whether, in this adaptation, they had their old meaning or assumed a new meaning and scope. The keenest analysis was applied to the institutions governed by those provisions to extract from them their precise nature. Then, the meaning of the law thus being fixed, the principles unraveled, we tried, with the resources furnished by logic and

---

131. See Levasseur supra note 9 at p.771–772.

juridical dialectic, to draw from them all the consequences that were there con-
tained in embryo, to foresee all the possible cases that could fall under their reg-
ulation. It was to this work that our elders and our teachers, the civilian scholars
of the first half of the nineteenth century, dedicated themselves.

From its side, practice, having as a rule the decisions of tribunals, ... worked
without respite on the interpretation of the Civil Code, a broader interpreta-
tion, more comprehensive than that of doctrinal writers, because it rested not
only on the articles but also outside the articles, when they had not provided
at all for the legal problems that arose. It did not proceed at all with a general
view and a methodical order. The facts posed the questions; the cases drew them
out, in the conflict of interests; and they had to be resolved. Undoubtedly, to
settle them, the judge was inspired by principles and lessons he had carried
from the Law School, and by opinions that doctrinal works furnished him. But
most often, neither the Faculty's courses nor the Scholar's page had foreseen the
specific difficulty that had to be resolved ... While guarding the integrity, the
impartiality which have always honored the judiciary of modern times, the
magistrate sees the cause alive before him and cannot be closed to considera-
tion of the moral or pecuniary interests involved therein. It is not an academic
case he studies, but it is two men, two of his fellow-men, between whom he
must decide.

The interpretation of the Civil Code by the tribunals could not always be the
same as that of the professors and writers. It is thus that case law has formed be-
side doctrine. But how could case law, thus understood, produce a true interpre-
tation of the Civil Code, an interpretation of the whole, which forms a body of
doctrine and harmonious synthesis? At the same time [...] another of our eld-
ers, M.Labbé, also entered upon a novel and fertile path. [...] He inaugurated
one of the first scientific and detailed annotation of important decisions, giving
them a value scope that they never had before. He was truly the master of the
genre. [...] Case law in its entirety, with partial divergences, such as doctrinal
writings also offer, forms a true system, harmonious and consistent.

It is not a dead legislation which the pages of the Civil Code contain. It is a
living law, which has already lived a long time, and which, I hope, is called to
live a long time yet. Hence, it had submitted itself and will submit itself to the
natural law of all that lives: it has transformed itself and will transform itself
even further. These transformations could only have been produced (where the
lawmaker did not intercede anew) by respecting the ancient texts, by softening
them through interpretation; but they were produced in numbers and in depth ...
The written law had to adapt to the new milieu. Now these transformations of
the civil law, what noted them down and at the same time consecrated them? It

is case law. Case law is the true expression of the civil law; it is the real and positive law, as long as it has not been changed. Thus, it, as much as the civil code itself, must be studied directly and scientifically."[132]

Julio C. Cueto-Rua, in a landmark article entitled "The Future of the Civil Law," wrote, *"The civilian method is rich and varied. It is not circumscribed, certainly, by the traditional dogma which reduces interpretation to the discovery of the 'real' intent of the legislator. Such a discovery, if possible at all, may help. But it is not decisive. The Civil Law method is not reduced, either, to the definition of the concepts of the law which will provide the premises for logical deductions. These are useful. They provide some degree of certainty and facilitate prediction of judicial behavior. But deduction is not the essential logical process in the application of the Civil Law. The field of methodology is, indeed, one of the most innovative areas of the Civil Law ... Civilian methodology in the interpretation of written general rules of law is not limited to a process of identification of the will of the legislator, nor is it bound by a strict theory of the sources of the law, which will restrict the jurist, and the judge, in their quest for the law applicable to a case, to codes or statutes as if they were the only available sources on which to rely, in order to show the objectivity of the adopted solution.... [T]he civilians have developed a variety of techniques and procedures in order to interpret codes and statutes, to 'fill the gaps in the law,' and to distribute justice between the parties. These techniques have shown their adequacy to solve the problems created by the accelerated process of social and political change ..."*[133]

In his treatise on "The Interpretation of Legislation in Canada," Pierre-André Côté wrote the following about the interpretation of the Civil Code of Québec:

*"First, the **Civil Code of Québec** establishes the jus commune for the subject matter it contains. For these subject matters (mainly private law), it is the law of principle: its function is equivalent to the common law in the other provinces ... In theory, because it is the **jus commune** and not exceptional law, the **Civil Code** must be interpreted liberally ... As statements of general law, subject to liberal interpretation, the rules set forth in the **Civil Code** may form the basis of reasoning by way of analogy; the judge can favour a dynamic rather than a static view of the enactment ...*

---

132. Shael Herman, A. Esmein., Loy. L. Rev 1971–72, XVIII, p.28–33. On case law and Labbé, see Appendix p.151: Arrêts and Arrêtistes.

133. Julio C. Cueto-Rua, *The Future of the Civil Law*, 37 La.L.Rev.645 et seq., 1977, p.658, 668.

The Preliminary Provision of the **Civil Code of Québec** *invites the interpreter to apply the rules in the Code to all subjects covered by both the letter and spirit of the law, and by the objects of the provisions ...*

'*It must be interpreted broadly so as to favour its spirit over its letter and enable the purpose of its provisions to be achieved ...*'[134]

Second, because of historical considerations of liberty and the free use of property, the interpretation of statutes was characterised by both formalism and strict interpretation. Interpretation in civil law has traditionally been less text-centric and more open to arguments based on extrinsic elements such as the Codifiers' Report or the writings of legal scholars; there is no reliance on restrictive principles of interpretation. The strict interpretation of provisions is limited to provisions of exception, which in some ways confirms the principle that general law can be extended to situations not formally envisaged in the text.

Third, differences also derive from the drafting style of the texts of civil law, rather than from the status of the **Civil Code** *and the liberal interpretation they command as a result. Legislative drafting techniques necessarily have an important influence on interpretation. Clearly, the Code is not drafted in typical statutory style. A text plainly and concisely setting forth certain general principles does not easily lend itself to a purely grammatical method of legislative interpretation. Other methods (contextual, purposive, historical) tend to be more appropriate. Thus, the style of legislative drafting will necessarily influence the choice of techniques of interpretation.*[135]

In the interpretation of civil law, and especially of the **Civil Code***, the historical method is absolutely fundamental. Above and beyond the texts (which, most often, do not establish new rules but rather give a new expression to old ones), the interpretative focus is on the entire tradition, a tradition which ultimately comes to us, through old French law, from Roman law. The case law of the Supreme Court nicely illustrates the importance given to the description and analysis of the historical sources of the rules and notions of the civil law.*"[136]

---

134. Doré v.Verdun (City of), 1997, 2.S.C.R. 862. 874.

135. Pierre-André Côté, *The Interpretation of Legislation in Canada*, 4th ed., Carswell, 2011, p.30–32.

136. *Id.* at p.459.

Chapter 2

Methods and Techniques/Means/ Tools of Interpretation

As seen above, by its very existence a statute or a code article lends itself to be interpreted. Because there is an indispensable "intermediary" between a statute or a code article as they have been written and their application or enforcement, there occurs inevitably an intellectual operation of "a subjective understanding and transposition" of the written text by the judge whose duties are to apply the law. Thereafter, the judge will endeavor to "objectively" understand the text of the law he is presented with by interpreting it in such a manner as to be able to fit the now-adjusted text to a given set of facts. In a sense, the process of interpretation is meant to enable the judge to adjust the "focus" of the law, to eliminate as much as possible any blurred vision that the judge could have from his subjective and personal understanding of the meaning of a statute or a code article. The judge should seek the help of a great variety of intellectual processes of interpretation to shed a rule of law from any ambiguity, doubt or controversy. The same intellectual processes of interpretation should be used by a judge should he be faced with a fact pattern which he may not be able to fit easily into a "legal garment" because of a potential "gap" in the written law. What to do if one can legitimately make the argument that there is no positive law on point, that there is a "lacuna" in the law? There exist some tools or techniques of interpretation that will safely guide the judge to investigate and search beyond the written letter of the law. As Portalis wrote in 1803–04 in his *Preliminary Speech*: "*How can one fetter the movement of time? ... Positive laws could never entirely replace the use of natural reason in the affairs of life ... ; the legislator cannot possibly provide for all eventualities ... When we are guided by nothing which is established or known, when what is involved is an absolutely new occurrence, we go back to principles of natural law.*

For if the lawmaker's foresight is limited, nature is infinite; she applies to all things that concern men ... The legislator's science consists in finding in each subject the principles most favorable to the common good; the judge's science is to put these principles into effect, to diversify them, to extend them, by means of wise and reasoned application, to private causes; to examine closely the spirit of the law when the letter kills."[137]

These last words we quoted from Portalis's speech will lead us to consider, on the one hand, the methods and techniques of interpretation in the context of the statutory law of the Civil Codes of France and Louisiana. To a greater extent, it will also allow us to examine the same methods and techniques of interpretation in the context of a few decisions of the Louisiana Supreme Court.

A. Methods and Techniques of Interpretation of Code Articles

In civil law jurisdictions, all methods of interpretation of statutory law, such as civil codes, are grounded on two fundamental premises. The first premise is that statutory law, as is a civil code, is the primary source of law. As Article 1 of the La. Civ. C. states: "The sources of law are legislation and custom." And Article 2 states that: "Legislation is a solemn expression of legislative will." Thus, the first responsibility for a judge who has to decide a case will be to search for and identify the statute(s) or civil code articles which appear to be the most likely to apply to the case. In this process, the judge will make a somewhat mechanical interpretation of the selected statute or code article by means of a hermeneutical analysis of the words and syntax of the statute or code article he has identified. The second premise is a logical and rational extrapolation of the first one as it directs the judge "to examine the spirit of the law where the letter kills."[138] In other words, as Articles 9 and 10 of the La. Civ. C. state:

Art. 9: *When a law is clear and unambiguous and its application does not lead to absurd consequences, the law shall be applied as written and no further interpretation may be made in search of the intent of the legislature.*

---

137. See Levasseur supra note 9 at p.769–770.
138. *Id.* at p.772.

Art. 10: *When the language of the law is susceptible of different meanings, it must be interpreted as having the meaning that best conforms to the purpose of the law.*

These two articles lead to looking at two broad methods of interpreting code articles: first, a method consisting in focusing on the "letter" of the law and, second, a method that invites the judge to look for the purpose of the law as his guiding principle and to search for the intent of the legislature.

Each one of these two methods provides the judge with a proper set of "tools" or techniques of interpretation.

1. Literal, Grammatical, Logical or "Ordinary" Method of Interpretation

This ordinary method of interpretation aims at extracting an exact and precise meaning of the text from the words chosen by the legislator, the grammatical structure of the sentences as well as the punctuation used in and in between the sentences. The rationale or justification for such an interpretation is that the text of the statute or the code article is the "expression of legislative will" (Art.2 La. Civ. C.) and that the will of the legislator is conveyed to the judge and "average reasonable person" by means of the words and sentences as they are laid down in the text.

a. *ad verbum or verbum verbo, literally*

A first type of such an interpretation could be called, in Latin, "**ad verbum**" or "**verbum verbo**," or "*exactly, literally*" in English. Such a kind of interpretation requires resorting to lexicological and philological techniques of analysis as well as having a particular awareness of the unique nature of legal linguistics or language of the law.

Where, for example, Article 86 of the La. Civ. C. states, "[m]arriage is a legal relationship between a man and a woman ..." an interpretation "**ad verbum**" would lead to comments of this kind:

(1) the use of the tense "is", which takes on an imperative form, combined with the words "**a man and a woman**" and, particularly, the word "**marriage**," leave no leeway for a court to look beyond the conjunction "**and**," as well as the two words "**man**" and "**woman**" given on either side of that conjunction before (2) the court "**must**" conclude that a "**marriage**" [and not a "partnership" or some "pact"], has been entered into (as long as the additional requirements of Art. 87 on marriage have been met) (3) In addition, the use of the present "**is**" of the verb "to be"

amounts to a direct instruction binding as such on the court. Art. 86 expresses a rule of law, which is a command, an order, for a court to follow.[139]

Likewise, Article 2590 tells us how to determine whether there is lesion or not: "If the sale was preceded by an option contract, or by a contract to sell, the property must be evaluated in the state in which it was at the time of that contract." A court cannot escape both the "**must**" and the "**was**" in such an article. The language of "*the law is clear and unambiguous and its application does not lead to absurd consequences ...*"[140]

Although the language of a civil code should be borrowed, to the largest extent, from the language spoken and written by the citizen for whom it is made, at times a particular and special legal language must be created to encompass situations or to refer to concepts which have meanings only in a tailored made legal language or legal linguistics. The concept of "*hypothec*" is a good illustration provided by Article 2393 of the French Civil Code: "*A hypothec is a real right in an immovable allocated to the discharge of an obligation. It is, by its nature, indivisible ...*"[141] Article 3280 of the Louisiana Civil Code defines a "mortgage" as "*an indivisible real right that burdens the entirety of the mortgaged property....*" As such it is also a "*right created over property to secure the performance of an obligation.*"[142] "Collation" is defined as "*the supposed or real return to the mass of the succession which an heir makes of property which he received in advance of his share or otherwise ...*" These words, "hypothec," "mortgage," and "collation" are words which have taken on a special and well-defined legal meaning and which, therefore, are not subject to any other interpretation than their "legalized or juridicalized" meaning. They are not used in the normal stream of the ordinary language.

At times the language of the law is not clear; it could be ambiguous or it can be "susceptible of different meanings" and in that case "*it must be interpreted as having the meaning that best conforms to the purpose of the law.*"[143] The purpose of the law will be determined by looking beyond the letter of the law and searching for the "will or intent" of the legislator or the "spirit of the law," as Portalis had urged the judge to do. This search for the "will or intent" of the

---

139. Thomas Aquinas, *Treatise on Law*, with an Introduction by Stanley Parry, Gateway, 1980; Question 92, "Of the Effect of Law."

140. La. Civ. C. art. 9.

141. Fr. Civ. C., site Legifrance, translation 2013 by A. Levasseur, Randall Trahan and David Gruning.

142. La. Civ. C. art. 3278.

143. La. Civ. C. art. 10.

legislator will lead to extracting the "**ratio legis**" or the *raison d'être/reason* for the existence of a statute or code article. Such can be done by making use of a variety of tools or techniques of interpretation all grounded on the core principle of "logic" as a method of reasoning.

Here are the prevalent techniques or methods of interpretation and reasoning that are the keys to unlocking the meaning of a statute or of a code article.

b. Interpreting a *generali sensu*

When a Code article is cast in broad terms, when there exists no restriction, no condition to take into account, the interpreter must then interpret that article in as general a sense as is possible. The interpreter cannot substitute himself to the legislator by adding requirements or conditions that are not in the text or reading distinctions or exceptions where none are suggested by the text.

Two code articles of the Louisiana Civil Code are illustrative of this method of interpretation or reasoning. One such article is Article 9: *"When a law is clear and unambiguous and its application does not lead to absurd consequences, the law shall be applied as written and no further interpretation may be made in search of the intent of the legislature."* The second article is Article 11: *"The words of a law must be given their generally prevailing meaning. Words of art and technical terms must be given their technical meaning when the law involves a technical matter."* For example, Article 102 of the French Civil Code provides that *"The domicile of a French person, as regards the exercise of his civil rights, is at the place where he has his main establishment."* Likewise, Article 38 of the La. Civ. C. states *"The domicile of a natural person is the place of his habitual residence ..."*

A French court could not focus on the words "French person" and rule that *only* French persons *"by birth,"* as opposed to French persons by naturalization, would fall under Article 102. Likewise, Article 38 of the La. Civ. C. could not be read by a Louisiana court to mean *only* "a male natural person" or an "American born natural person." Of interest, and sometimes puzzling, to "some" students of Louisiana Law is Article 215 of the Civil Code which states: *"A child, whatever be his age, owes honor and respect to his father and mother."* When a twenty-three- or twenty-five-year-old law student is asked the question whether he/she considers himself/herself a "child" under this Article 215, there is often some hesitation in their answers. That is, until we point out that the text of the "law" of article 215 makes no distinction on account of age and it is therefore pretty clear that each one of them must qualify himself/herself as a "child" and "whatever be his/her age." Furthermore, the words "father" and "mother" are not "restricted" in any way, neither on account of "age" nor on account of "blood relationship," i.e., whether the father and/or mother are the natural or adoptive father and/or mother. No exception! No distinction!

What is perhaps most surprising and bewildering to many law students of "Torts" is that the same law of "civil liability" or "*delicts*" is stated in a few and simple code articles which incorporate fundamental principles as opposed to being laid down under the form of detailed rules as tort cases provide. Consider the statement made in Paragraph A of Article 2315 of the La. Civ. C. or in the identical Article 1382 of the Fr. Civ. C.: "*Every act whatever of man that causes damage to another obliges him by whose fault it happened to repair it.*" Notice that the first two words are common words, words of the ordinary language, which ought to be understood as such. It is also worthy to note how broad and general those words, such as "every," are! No distinction is made between "physical," "material," or "psychological" acts; neither is a distinction made between the kinds of acts that could "*cause damage to another*"; is it a physical act? an immoral act? a direct or indirect act? No adjective has been added by the legislator because what needed to be formally stated at the outset was a "principle," which was that one who causes a damage to another should "compensate" that other and, thus, should not go unpunished.

The above examples stand for the proposition that when the text of the law is "general," "broad," or "all inclusive," no distinction can be made. This method of reasoning was known in Roman law in the form of the maxim: "**Ubi lex non distinguit, nec nos distinguere debemus.**"

c. *Interpreting or Reasoning a contrario sensu*

The *Dictionary of the Civil Code*[144] gives the following definition of this method of reasoning: "*Reasoning consisting in acknowledging that a case opposite/contrary to the case contemplated in a text, is excluded by that text and subject to an opposite rule. Qui dicit de uno, de altero negat: what is said about one thing is denied about another.*"

Whenever a code article lays down a rule of law for a given hypothesis in a somewhat restrictive or particular manner such as, for example, when it creates an obligation for a well identified person or group of persons, or when a particular rule of law is said to apply to a particular set of facts as when it appears to lay down the law for an exception, it will logically follow that a dif-

---

144. *Dictionary of the Civil Code*, LexisNexis, 2014.

ferent and even opposite rule of law or obligation will be controlling a different, and even more opposite, class or group of persons or a different, opposite, set of facts. Article 1165 of the French Civil Code states, in part, that *"Agreements produce effects between the contracting parties only."* The adverb "only" is *"restrictive"* in meaning and suffices by itself to justify using an **a contrario sensu** reasoning that would lead one to say that a class of persons other than the parties to the agreement, i.e., third parties, cannot be subjected to the "effects" of a contract to which they are not parties. It is therefore the reason why the same Code Article 1165 goes on to say: *"... they do not harm a third party, and they benefit him only in the case provided for in Article 1121."*[145]

Article 1983 of the Louisiana Civil Code bears also on "the effects of contracts" but, because it is not as explicit as the French Code Article 1165, it lends itself to a much more convincing reasoning **a contrario sensu**. Article 1983 states, in part, that *"[c]ontracts have the effect of law for the parties."* An **a contrario sensu** reasoning will lead to stating an opposite rule of law as far as "third parties," another class of persons than the "parties" to the contract, are concerned; that opposite rule of law would then become: *"a contract between parties can have no effect of law for third parties."* This "made-up" rule of law is then perfectly compatible with the law of Article 1985, which states that *"[c]ontracts may produce effects for third parties only when provided by law."* In other words, reasoning **a contrario sensu** on this Article 1985, we would say that if "a contract may produce effects for third parties," **a contrario sensu** that contract cannot produce effects "against" third parties, and it cannot cause a detriment to non-parties, which is basically the law laid down in Article 1983.

Article 27 of the Louisiana Civil Code can be used as a "ground" for an **a contrario sensu** reasoning. The Article states that *"[a]ll natural persons enjoy general legal capacity to have rights and duties."* The "facts" in this short article are "all natural persons" and the law is "enjoy general capacity to have rights and duties." If we take a different and even opposite set of facts than those given in the article, we will have to reach a different and even opposite rule of law by an **a contrario sensu** reasoning. Thus a "made up" rule of law would be: *"legal or juridical persons do not enjoy general capacity to have rights and duties."*

Much more explicit in this respect is Article 2589 which states, in part, that *"[l]esion can be claimed <u>only</u> by the seller and <u>only</u> in sales of corporeal immovables."* (emphasis ours). One will have noticed the dual use of "<u>only</u>," making the

---

145. Fr. Civ. C. art. 1121 provides for a stipulation for the benefit of another. See P. Raymond Lamonica and Jerry G. Jones, *Louisiana Legislative Law and Procedures Companion Handbook*, Thomson West, 2012, at p.204 on "Expressio unius est exclusio alterius."

"facts" and the "law" of this Article "doubly" restrictive. Thus, an **a contrario sensu** reasoning would lead to denying to a "buyer" the right to claim lesion and a second **a contrario** reasoning would lead to a "dual" **a contrario** outcome: where the article refers to "corporeal immovables," we would have to exclude from the scope of application of lesion both "corporeal movables" and "incorporeal immovables." Where the Code Article "includes" a particular item, it "excludes" another. Such is the meaning of the Latin maxim: "*inclusio unius, exclusio alterius.*"

There are alternative forms of saying the same thing as "a contrario sensu": one can use the above Latin maxim: *inclusio unius, exclusio alterius,* the inclusion of one implies the exclusion of the other, or another Latin maxim: *Qui dicit de uno, de altero negat,* to say something about one thing is to deny it about another or, still, a third maxim "exceptio est strictissimae interpretationis," an exception is of the most restrictive interpretation.

d. Reasoning *ratione legis stricta*

"**Ratio legis**" is the "reason for the law" (in the sense of "lex," statutory law) or the intent that induced the legislator into using a certain terminology and a certain grammatical syntax in writing a statute or code articles as it did. *"For courts and for advocates, an understanding of the elements of the legislative process can be of central importance when judicial decisions may be predicated upon a determination of what was 'intended' by the legislature in the wording of an enactment."*[146] Indeed, behind the words that we read an intricate intellectual, linguistic and legistics process took place to mold and frame the statute/code article in the form we are handed. Behind the words we read, we must endeavor to access the reason that prompted the legislator to choose those words and why they were meant to be incorporated in the statute or the code article. In other words, it can be decisive in determining the meaning of a statute or a code article, to find out why "this word" rather than "another" became the expression of the legislator's will.

After we have identified that reason or will of the legislator, we must insert it into the written and lifeless statement we read to instill in that language the "spirit," the "soul" that the selected written words were meant to have. In this process, we are interpreting the "law" against the background of its "reason."

In some instances that "ratio/reason" must be understood strictly or narrowly. In this case one must consider the intent of the legislator as laying down a justified rational limitation to the application of a certain rule of law. As a

---

146. *Id.* at p.175.

consequence, in those instances where the "reason for applying that restrictive law" does not exist because those instances do not fit the narrowly and restrictively defined fact pattern of the words of the rule of law, one will be prohibited from "forcing" that rule of law onto the "outside of the words of the law," or not contemplated and not provided for the new fact pattern. Thus, if logic instructs us that there is no "reason" that could justify applying that restrictively stated rule of law as directed by a narrowly described fact pattern, because it would be going against that "reason," then, where the reason for applying a rule of law ceases to exist, the rule of law itself cannot have any existence. Thus the Latin maxim: *cessante ratione legis, cessat lex.* The judge and/or the jurist will then turn to one or more other logical methods of reasoning or extrinsic methods of reasoning, such as the free scientific research method.

Let us illustrate the use of this method of reasoning "**ratione legis stricta**" with some examples of code articles.

When a text of statutory law lays down a list of conditions or requirements for the existence of a certain right, or the validity of some well-defined juridical act, that text of law should be considered as a warning signal to the reader, judge or jurist, to the effect that there is or there are reasons behind the listing which, very likely, will not allow for reading any additional or different condition(s) or requirement(s) to that rule of law.

For example: Article 3072 of the La. Civ. C. states, in part, that "*A compromise shall be made in writing or recited in open court.*" The "reason" for such a strict requirement of form, "in writing," is that "*a compromise is a contract whereby the parties, through concessions made by one or more of them, settle a dispute or an uncertainty concerning an obligation or other legal relationship.*" Furthermore, "*A compromise precludes the parties from bringing a subsequent action based upon the matter that was compromised.*"[147] The purpose of the writing is therefore to make sure that the parties understand what they are doing, and that this "solemnity" of the writing will focus their attention on the seriousness of the juridical act they are about to enter into. That specific reason behind the law must therefore be understood strictly so as to deny the existence of a compromise if there is no writing.

We have seen above that "[l]esion can be claimed only by the seller and only in sales of corporeal immovables,"[148] and that reasoning a contrario sensu leads to denying that right of lesion to a buyer. But behind this strictly limited rule

---

147. La. Civ. C. Art. 3080.
148. La. Civ. C. Art. 2589.

of law on lesion, there is a reason or there are reasons which, in the mind of the legislator, required that this right be restricted to the seller and, furthermore, that the exercise of that right be restricted by a series of requirements such as the exercise of that right being "*brought within a peremptive period of one year from the time of the sale*"[149] or that the right of the seller to rescind the sale for lesion is triggered only "*when the price is less than one half of the fair market value of the immovable.*"[150] Why such a restrictive right of the seller? One reason is that a seller of his "corporeal immovable" ought to know what the "market" value of "his" immovable is before he puts it on the market, and if he makes a mistake he should be the only one to blame. Another reason is given by the history of lesion which was included in the French Civil Code of 1804 for the purpose of protecting, to the extent of 7/12th of the value of an immovable (land, at that time), the nobility, which was under a lot of pressure and stress after the Revolution, to sell their "landed estates" to the Bourgeoisie and the bankers at the time. Lesion was then justified as being the consequence or result of either a lack of free consent on the part of the seller (somehow forced to sell under the circumstances of the time), or the consequence of some vice of consent such as "error," particularly error as to the value of the immovable sold. This reason, or these reasons, justify restricting the right of lesion to the seller of an immovable since it was believed in 1804 in France and in 1808–1825 in Louisiana, that (1), a buyer, is never "forced" to buy an immovable, or (2) that if a buyer buys a corporeal immovable at a price below 7/12th or half its value (moiety), it is because the seller made an error as to the value of the immovable he sold. In either case the sale could be rescinded.

One will have noticed with the example of "lesion" that two methods of reasoning could be used on the same code article. They were: **a contrario sensu** (reasoning on "words") and **ratione legis stricta** (reasoning on the basis of the "reason behind the words"). This is not unusual; actually it is common and even highly recommended to use two or three compatible methods of reasoning so as to add strength and persuasiveness to one's legal argument. We will provide examples of such an approach further down as we go further in this survey of the methods of reasoning and, above all, in our analysis of some landmark decisions of the Louisiana Supreme Court.

A third example of reasoning ratione legis stricta (as well as a contrario sensu) is taken from La. Civ .C. Art. 1493(A) that states, in part, as follows: "*Forced heirs are descendants of the first degree who, at the time of the death of*

---

149. La. Civ. C. Art. 2595
150. La. Civ. C. Art. 2589

the decedent, are twenty three years of age or younger ..." The reasons behind
the restrictive statement of this rule of law can be found in the concepts of
family, heir and patrimony in the civil law. The civil law family includes "*all
the persons who are united by the bond of blood, who have the same ancestor*"
and, more narrowly, "*the limited group of the father, mother and their children
(under age), living with them (nuclear family).*"[151] The concept of heir is defined, "*in a strict sense, as a legal or natural relative called by law to the succession of a deceased; is contrasted both, in his status as heir ... to the legatee (called
by testament) and as heir by blood (relative) to the spouse entitled to inherit and
other successors.*"[152] Patrimony is understood as "*the aggregate of the assets,
claims, obligations of one person (that is to say, his rights and charges which can
be valued in money); both the assets and liabilities, considered as forming a universality, a whole including not only a person's present assets but also his future
assets.*"[153] So the reasons behind "forced heirship" are to keep the "patrimony"
of the deceased in the "family," to "reserve,"[154] this patrimony to the "descendants of the first degree" in that family as these descendants are presumed to
continue the "person" of the deceased and to limit the right of these descendants to that age, twenty three in Louisiana, when they should be "on their
own." Louisiana law and French law have maintained, with some adjustments
over the last decades, this concept of "forced heirship" whereas the Province
of Québec does not recognize it. Different societies, albeit belonging to the
civil law system, may have different beliefs, aspirations and "reasons" behind
their rules of law; hence the importance of relating written rules of law to the
"reason(s)" which justify and explain the words in which the rules are stated.

e. *Reasoning pro **subjecta materia***

Meaning, literally: reasoning according to the subject matter. As Article 10
of the La. Civ. C. states: "*When the language of the law is susceptible of different meanings, it must be interpreted as having the meaning that best conforms to
the purpose of the law.*" And as Article 12 further provides: "*When the words of*

---

151. The word "family" in English is "**famille**" in French: see *Dictionary of the Civil Code*,
A. Levasseur, LexisNexis 2014.

152. The word "heir" in English is "héritier" in French: see *Dictionary of the Civil Code*,
A. Levasseur, LexisNexis 2014.

153. The word "patrimony" in English is "patrimoine" in French: see *Dictionary of the
Civil Code*, A. Levasseur, LexisNexis 2014.

154. "Réserve" or "réserve héréditaire" is that "portion of a succession reserved by law
to certain héritiers réservatairesñ forced heirs ..."; see *Dictionary of the Civil Code*, A. Levasseur, LexisNexis 2014.

a law are ambiguous, their meaning must be sought by examining the context in which they occur and the text of the law as a whole." Thus, in interpreting **pro subjecta materia**, one must take into consideration the particular place or location of the text that one must interpret within the broader "subject matter" in which the text is located. For example, the word "child" is often mentioned in the Civil Code. We have seen above, under a **generali sensu**, that this word "child," because of its location in Article 215, must be given a "broad interpretation" as it is mentioned under a series "*of the duties of legitimate children towards their parents*" (sub-title of Section 1, Chapter 5 Of Parental Authority). A legitimate child is "legitimate" until death regardless of his/her age. But if we look at the same word "child" in art. 1493(A), we must then read the word "child" according to the subject matter of "Donations" (Title 2) and the narrower subject matter of "The Disposable Portion and Its Reduction in Case of Excess" (Chapter 3). The meaning of "child" then becomes a "*forced heir who [is] a descendant of the first degree who, at the time of the death of the decedent, [is] twenty-three years of age or younger.*" The meaning of "child" here is obviously different from its meaning in Article 215. And what about the meaning of "child" in Article 2318 according to which " *[t]he father and the mother are responsible for the damage occasioned by their minor child, who resides with them …*"? A "child" under Article 2318 is a natural person under the age of eighteen who resides with his father and mother; so, a "child" under the law *Of Offenses and Quasi-Offenses,* may not be a "child" under Article 1493(A) but will be a child "forever" under Article 215. Another illustration, among many other possibilities, of this method of reasoning is provided by Articles 2475 and 2477 of the La. Civ. C. both under the *Obligations of the Seller* in a contract of "Sale." Reasoning on the meaning of "delivery" will vary according to the nature or subject matter of the "thing" to be delivered. If the "thing" to be "delivered" is an immovable, that subject matter instructs us that the delivery "*is deemed to take place upon execution of the writing that transfers its ownership.*"[155] If the thing to be delivered is a "movable," the delivery "*takes place by handing it over to the buyer.*" As shown, "delivery" will take on a different meaning according to the subject matter of the contract of sale.

f. Reasoning in **pari materia**

Article 13 of the La. Civ. C. states that "*[l]aws on the same subject matter must be interpreted in reference to each other.*" The assumption one is making in using this method of interpretation is that the legislator intended to take

---

155. La. Civ. C. art. 2477-1.

into account legislation already in existence that addresses a subject matter of the same kind, same matter. This method of interpretation is particularly appropriate when a subsequent statutory act is passed on a subject matter that is similar, in substance, to the subject matter of statutory acts already in force. As Article 13 states above, a subsequent statute on the "*same subject matter (as a preexisting statute) must be interpreted in reference to each other.*"[156] For example, Article 2293 of the La. Civ. C. instructs us that "*[a] management of affairs is subject to the rules of mandate to the extent those rules are compatible with management of affairs.*" Due to the close resemblance between the matters of "mandate" and "management of the affairs of another," the rules of the contract of mandate will apply when compatible with the management of the affairs of another. In fact, the institution of the management of the affairs of another was created in the absence of a contract of "mandate." The same is true of the contract of exchange and the contract of sale, so much so that Article 2464 provides that "*[t]he contract of exchange is governed by the rules of the contract of sale, with the differences provided in this Title.*" As another example, we can cite Article 1228 on "Collation by descendants." Paragraph B of this article invites us to treat "legal heirs" like "testamentary heirs" whenever "*children … must collate what they have received … by donation inter vivos.*" The subject matters of "legal heirship" and "testamentary heirship" are so similar that the same rules on collation must apply.

g. Reasoning *ab inutilitate legis et ab absurdum*

This is a tricky and difficult method of reasoning to use because it goes against the assumption that "*legislation is not a pure act of power; it is an act of wisdom, justice and reason*"[157] or, as Article 2 of the La. Civ. C. states, that " *legislation is a solemn expression of legislative will.*" So, a statute is presumed to make sense, to be reasonable and if it is "*clear and unambiguous and its application does not lead to absurd consequences, the law shall be applied as written.*" Thus, the legislator is presumed to be reasonable, fair, just and "incapable" of enacting statutes the application of which would render the statute "useless" or, worst, "absurd." The same is true in matters of contract as illustrated by Article 2049 according to which "*[a] provision susceptible of different meanings must be interpreted with a meaning that renders is effective and not with one that renders it ineffective.*"

We have used, above, Articles 2315(A) of the La. Civ. C. and Article 1382 of the French Civil Code to illustrate the method of reasoning a **generali sensu**.

---

156. See Lamonica supra note 144 at p.203, "*ejusdem generis.*"
157. See Levasseur supra note 9 at p.767.

We can now use the same code articles to illustrate an application of the reasoning "**ab inutilitate et ab absurdum.**" Article 2315(A) reads: "*Every act whatever of man that causes damage to another obliges him by whose fault it happened to repair it.*" For an "**ab inutilitate**" or an "**ab absurdum**" reasoning one must focus on the words "*whatever act*" plus "*causes damage*" plus "*fault ... to repair it.*" Indeed, one can ask the following question: What if the "*whatever act*" took place and a "*damage*" occurred as a result but the "*fault,*" if there was one objectively, was actually the result of re-acting in self-defense or prompted by a combination of a fortuitous event with an act of man? Wouldn't it be absurd to hold the tortfeasor, the "man" who caused the damage, liable and obliged to "repair," when there was no legal fault on his part because of the lack of intent or negligence in causing a "damage to another"? If the "law" were to the contrary, that law could be considered "useless" or "absurd." In addition, if we look into the reason or purpose for that code article, that law, as we will do in a section below, it would be easy to make the argument that the legislator could not have meant to hold liable a person who acted in self-defense and, as a result, caused a damage to another, to the same extent and for the "same reason" as a person who meant to act so as to cause a damage to another. As we will further discussed below, this kind of reasoning based on "words" and the reason behind these words can be identified with the maxim: "**cessante ratione legis, cessat lex,**" meaning where the reason for the law ceases to exist, the law itself ceases to exist.

We could take La. Civ. C. Article 236 as another example of a reasoning **ab absurdum** or **ab inutilitate legis** and focus again on some words of that article. Article 236 states that: "*Fathers and mothers may justify themselves in an action begun against them for assault and battery, if they acted in defense of the persons of their children.*" We can make two observations on this article: first, is it not "logical" and "reasonable" to relate this article to the code article we just analyzed and interpreted, i.e., Article 2315? It is logical because we have a father or a mother who are "acting" in the place of a child incapable of "acting" and when doing so the father or mother "*caused damage to another.*" And when we call on the "reason" behind both Articles 236 and 2315, we can only conclude that there was "no fault" on the part of the father or mother because one or the other "*acted in the defense of the persons of their children.*" Furthermore to hold a father or mother liable when they acted "violently" in defense of their children would be in conflict with the words of and the reason behind Article 235 which states in the imperative form that "*[f]athers and mothers owe protection to their children ...*"

One will have noticed here that in reasoning on the above code articles we have made use of at least two methods of reasoning, one based on the words of the articles, and one based on the "reason" or "purpose" of the same articles. The science of interpreting code articles is dictated by the science of codification. The two are intertwined. One must fully understand how and why to "codify" is an art and a particular technique at drafting. Only when that art or technique of drafting is fully comprehended and grasped, is one then in possession of the tools necessary to make the law of a code "*a living law.*"[158]

It will be one conclusion and, at the same time, a strong recommendation, of this survey of methods of reasoning that one should resort to at least two methods of reasoning to undertake a sound and reliable interpretation of any code article or statutory law. One method should be based on the words of the code article or the statute, and the second should be based on the "ratio/reason/purpose" that justifies the code article or the statute under analysis. The two methods will work *in tandem*; they will strengthen each other. A second conclusion one will draw from this survey of methods of reasoning is that to one method of reasoning there is, most likely, a counter method of reasoning. We will come across some illustrations of this second conclusion when we dissect the cases given below and point out what method of reasoning the Court used here or there. A logical process of analysis will lead to the identification of a counter method of reasoning for each method of reasoning used by the Court in providing the grounds for its decision. In this respect, the Courts should heed the informed and learned advice of Portalis who told the judges who were about to apply the brand new completed French Civil Code, that their "*science is to put the(se) principles into effect* [such as the principles given in La. civ. code articles 235–236, 2315], *to diversify them, and to extend them, by means of wise and reasoned application, to private causes; to examine closely the spirit of the law when the letter kills[…].*"[159]

As Esmein wrote, "*it is not a dead legislation which the pages of the Civil Code contain. It is a living law, which has already lived a long time, and which, I hope, is called to live a long time yet. Hence, it had submitted and will submit to the natural law of all that lives; it has transformed itself and will transform itself even further. These transformations could only have been produced (where the lawmaker did not intercede anew) by respecting the ancient texts, by softening them through interpretation; but they were produced in numbers and in depth … The written law had to adapt to the new milieu. Now, these transformations of the*

---

158. Law Reform Commission of Canada, Criminal Law, *Towards a Codification*, Study Paper, Ohara, 1976. On " *ab inutilitate legis et ab absurdum,*" see Lamonica supra note 144 at p.193.

159. See Levasseur supra note 9 at p.772.

civil law, what noted them down and at the same time consecrated them? It is case law. Case law is the true expression of the civil law; it is the real and positive law, as long as it has not been changed. Thus, it, as much as the civil code itself, must be studied directly and scientifically."[160]

h. Reasoning *ab auctoritate*

This method of reasoning is a logical and necessary consequence of what we attempted to make clear in the first part of this book: the civil law "judge" and the civil law "jurist" have always had an important constructive role to play in the "[m]aking of the civil law."[161] They are located on each side of the bases of the isosceles triangle, which we used to illustrate the close cooperation in the roles played by the three basic sources of law in civil law: legislation, jurisprudence and doctrine.

This method of reasoning is simple to use and, may be for that reason, not as strong a method of reasoning as most others. In other words, it is advisable to use this method of reasoning in conjunction with others. The reason being that when using an **ab auctoritate** method of reasoning one is relying on the authority attached to a "court decision" or to a "legal scholar's opinion." Relying on the authority of a prior court decision is the standard method of interpretation at common law, which is controlled by the principle of **stare decisis** or the theory of "precedent." At civil law, for reasons easy to understand, the prevailing principle, as we have seen above, is that of **jurisprudence constante**. This means that a series of cases all adopting the same understanding of a rule of law and, therefore, all reaching the same legal conclusion, will lead to the expectation that, in the future, the same legal conclusion on the same rule of law will prevail. There must indeed exist continuity in the rule of law and in the case law, *"so that it becomes necessary, in some way, to judge today much as we judged yesterday, and that there be no variations between judicial decisions other than those resulting from the progress of enlightenment and the force of circumstances ... If there is no precise provision on a particular matter, then ... an unbroken line of similar decisions ... takes the place of enacted law."*[162] So, lawyers will not or should not hesitate to refer to cases in their briefs and in the presentation of their oral legal arguments before a court. It may be common for a Louisiana court to refer to prior existing cases and to rely on their authority,

---

160. A. Esmein, translation by Shael Herman, *Case Law and Doctrine*, 18 Loy. L. Rev. 23–37 (1971–72), at p.32–33.

161. Alan Watson, *The Making of the Civil Law*, Harvard University Press, 1981.

162. See Levasseur supra note 9 at p.770–771.

because Louisiana is a mixed jurisdiction. On the other hand, a French court decision, a decision from the Cour de Cassation in particular, will not mention a case in the body of the decision because the only source of law a French court can refer to is legislation. However, in researching the issues of law raised by a case, the judges will look back at the existing jurisprudence on these issues, just as the judges will look at the writings of legal scholars on these same legal issues, all with the motivation of "*judging today as they had judged yesterday.*" If they have to deviate from existing decisions, they will make sure that they can rely on scholarly "opinions or writings," as well as on accepted creative methods of interpretation of statutory provisions.

Besides the courts' decisions or case law, the history of the civil law has established very clearly that in the making of the civil law, legal scholars have played a major role and contributed substantially to the very nature of the civil law tradition. As Portalis again stated:

"*It is fortunate that the study of case law is a science that attracts talent, enhances self-respect, and awakens emulation ... If there is no precise provision on a particular matter, then ... an opinion or an accepted maxim takes the place of enacted law ... Interpretation by way of doctrine consists in grasping the true sense of the laws, applying them in a discerning fashion, and supplementing them in those cases which the laws have not provided for. Without this kind of interpretation could we think of fulfilling the judge's function?*" We will see, in the next section, that Louisiana courts do include references to the writings of doctrinal writers in the civil law as persuasive sources of law. In this respect, there are references, of course, to writers of the civil law of Louisiana but also to writers of the civil law of France, Québec ...

It is worth pointing out here that the writing of "case notes" is not so much a common law creation as it is a civil law creation. The "case note" is the perfect illustration of the symbiosis or the harmonious and close relationship between courts and doctrine in the civil law system. This innovation of writing case notes on court decisions has been attributed to Labbé who "*inaugurated one of the first scientific and detailed annotations of important decisions, giving them a value and scope that they had never had before. He was truly the master of the genre.*"[163]

i. Reasoning *a rubrica*

This is not a recommended method of reasoning because it is not very "legal" or "legalistic" in its application. One could refer to this method of rea-

---

163. See Esmein supra note 160 at p.32. On Labbé see the Appendix in this book.

soning as a method of "last resort." For instance, it could be used in the event one is unable to find any other one or two methods of reasoning which, as discussed above, would be much more convincing because of the support these other methods of reasoning would find in the words or, better, in the reason of the code article or the statute under analysis.

Very simply, this method consists in saying that the title or heading of a legislative text defines the extent of its meaning and of its interpretation. It assumes that the title of a statutory law or of a section or chapter in a civil code, has so close a relationship with the subject matter of that law that the title or heading basically restricts the interpretation of the law or the code article itself to the narrow meaning of the words of that heading. Any reading beyond the narrow meaning of the words of the heading or title would be a violation of the law itself. Such a method of reasoning could find grounds for application in some specialized and technical fields of law such as tax law, criminal law, civil procedure but it has no place in a civil code. Actually, Louisiana Revised Statute 1: 13 states very clearly that:

"A. Headings to sections, source notes, ... are given for the purpose of convenient reference and do not constitute part of the law."

j. *Travaux Préparatoires;* **Preparatory Works**

From a common law point of view, in *Statutes and Statutory Construction*[164] we read that *"[h]istorical information is an important source of insight and enlightenment about most human affairs ... [T]he criterion of decision, legislative intent or statutory meaning, serves as the principle for making judgments on the relevance of historical information. More kinds of detailed information are relevant to a decision based upon the intent criterion than to a decision based upon the accepted meaning ... Legislative history is often ambiguous and inconclusive, supporting the view that when a court purports to decide a statutory construction issue on historical grounds it is in fact indulging in judicial legislation in judging the pertinence and probative force of the historical evidence ... It is established practice in American legal processes to consider relevant information concerning the historical background of enactment in making decisions about how a statute is to be construed and applied ... These extrinsic aids may show the circumstances under which the statute was passed, the mischief at which it was aimed and the object it was supposed to achieve ... The legal history of a statute, including prior statutes on the same subject, is a valuable guide for determining what object an*

---

164. Norman J. Singer, *Statutes and Statutory Construction,* 4th ed., Callaghan, 1984.

act is supposed to achieve ... The events occurring immediately prior to the time when an act becomes law comprises an instructive source, indicative of what meaning the legislature intended. Therefore, the history of events during the process of enactment, from its introduction in the legislature to its final validation, has generally been the first extrinsic aid to which courts have turned in attempting to construe an ambiguous act ..."[165]

In the Civil Code of Louisiana, Article 9 instructs the "interpreter" as follows: *"when a law is unclear and ambiguous,"* interpretation may be made by searching for the intent of the legislature. And as Article 10 states a law must be interpreted as having the meaning that best conforms to the purpose of the law. The search for the "intent of the legislature" and interpreting a statute so as to conform to its "purpose," are directives given to *"the judge and the jurist, imbued with the general spirit of the laws"* so that they will make a direct application of the statute.[166] It is, to a large extent, in the "history" of a statute and its "preparatory works" that the judge and the jurist must turn to find guidance in their interpretation of the statute or code article under consideration. This process, this method of interpretation, is shared by the common law and the civil law.

As regards the civil law system in general, it has been written that the *"preparatory works are the actual leaven of the statute ... It is in their close analysis that one may best discover the ratio legis ... The exposé des motifs, the statement of purpose, the successive drafts of the text, the content of the reports, the amendments adopted or rejected enlighten the overall atmosphere and spirit which have been those of the text eventually passed and which may help in making a choice between one interpretation or another ... However, it must be pointed out that in these preparatory works one will find only pointers, guides, often conflicting with each other, and that however valuable they may be, they still do not have any binding force for the court. They are methods of interpretation ab auctoritate and help support a reasonable meaning to a text ... but, per se, they are denied any normative value."*[167]

"The interpreter is fully justified in consulting the preamble of a statute or the exposé des motifs. The legislature is presumed to have disclosed in the motifs the true reasons or purpose for the statute. The interpreter, acting cautiously, may also look into the travaux préparatoires/the preparatory works (reports submitted on behalf

---

165. *Id.* at p.283–302 #48.02 to 48.04. See also Lamonica supra note 145 at p.209 et seq. and 218 et seq.

166. See Levasseur supra note 9 at p.769.

167. Jean-Louis Bergel, *Méthodologie Juridique*, Presses Universitaires de France, at p.242–243 [author's translation].

of the commissions before the parliamentary assemblies; parliamentary debates). The interpreter is also invited, if the rule has any past history, to find some inspiration and guidance in the historical interpretation of the controversial text (it may be useful to go back to Domat or Pothier to elucidate texts which have been inspired by their works); optima est legum interpres consuetudo-custom is the best interpretation of the law."[168] As the Louisiana Supreme Court ruled in 1974, *"The text (of then La.Civ.C.Art.2321) unequivocally proves: 'the owner of an animal is answerable ...' The legislative exposé des motifs and reports of the owner's liability for damages caused by his things or animals show the reason to be because the damage is imputed to his lack of care and because, moreover, nothing that belongs to one person should be able to harm another without making reparation for it. 13 Locre, La Legislation Civile, Commerciale et Criminelle de la France 43 (1827); 13 Fenet, Travaux Préparatoires du Code Civil 476–77 (1836)."*[169]

2. Extrinsic Methods of Interpretation or Reading "Beyond the Civil Code"[170]

As useful as the above methods of reasoning or methods interpretation are from a logical as well as exegetical perspective, they remain somewhat restricted to the text of a statute or code article and to the reason or purpose that led the legislature to adopt that statute or code article. Yet, as Saleilles wrote in his preface to François Gény's **Méthode d'Interprétation et Sources en Droit Privé Positif** (June 1899): *"When the social environment has changed and new ideas have appeared—although the eternal principles of justice have not been modified or altered—the continued application of the law takes place under completely different conditions ... It was necessary for the law to adjust itself to this new world in order to satisfy these new concepts of justice. Although the substance of justice continues immutable, it can remain just only if it adapts itself to the emerging economic and social changes ... Assuming that the legislative intent has not reached beyond the foreseen and expressed solutions and their most immediate consequences, everything else—the almost infinite complex or related questions which have to be resolved—requires a method extraneous to the inquiry into the legislative intent and the development of systematic and precise procedures toward the formulation of rules ... We have witnessed the formation of a more delicate and more flexible method, better harmonized with life, which is a rational method*

---

168. Gérard Cornu, *Droit Civil, Introduction au droit*, 13éme éd., Monchrestien, 2007, at page 206 #393 [author's translation].

169. Holland v. Buckley, 305 So.2d 113, La.1974.

170. René David, *The Civil Code in France To-Day*, 34 La. L. Rev., 1974, p.911.

in the proper sense, not a purely syllogistic method of reasoning. It is rational because it requests from reason not the fabrication of syllogisms, but the discovery of solutions which are harmonious with equity and practical necessities while still being within the scope of a broad, flexible construction of the statutory texts."[171] In a sense, whenever we look at the text of a statute or at a code article as laying down a meaning that is self-sufficient, autonomous and setting its own outer limits of application, we are confining and restricting ourselves to look only "inward." There are, however, additional and long recognized methods of interpretation that provide the interpreter with the means of looking forward, of projecting the text of a statute or of a code article into the future; one is encouraged to look *"through the Civil Code; but beyond the Civil Code."*[172]

In his Introduction to Gény's *Méthode d'Interprétation et Sources en Droit Privé Positif*, Jayro Mayda wrote the following about François Gény's "libre recherche scientifique," or "free scientific research": *"The practical key is Gény's insistence on strict statutory interpretation ex tunc to open the door to judicial creation of rules by the free-search method, unencumbered by the fiction of finding ex nunc a non-existent or necessary different intent of the original legislator. On the whole, Gény's purpose and tone are critical and destructive of the established positivism and exegetic method—the construction upon the legislative text of a system of concepts manipulated by formal syllogism in an autonomous context, independent of the world of facts ... Gény's achievements, as appreciated by subsequent writers, can be conveniently clustered into several interrelated groupings.*

1.   Gény's signaled the beginning of a process of reexamination which ended the monopoly of legislated law; but while indicating 'gaps in positive law, did not convert the whole legal system into one big gap.'

2.   He overcame the dogmatism of the exegetic school, the abstract formalism of the traditional method, and was the harbinger of a new anti-positivism.

3.   He led the attack on the mechanical interpretation of the [codes] and criticized the conceptual acrobats stretching the enacted rules by dry logic.

4.   He demonstrated the uses [of] an ancient text to handle the most modern cases; assigned the interpreter a central place in the life of the law which takes

---

171. Gény, *Méthode d'Interprétation et Sources en Droit Privé Positif*, an English translation by the Louisiana State Law Institute, Preface by Raymon Saleilles, at p.LXXVI.

172. In the Preface to Gény's work, Raymond Saleilles wrote, "I could not end with better words than those inspired by an analogous phrase of Ihering, which is the focal point of the whole book of Mr. Gény: 'Through the Civil Code, but beyond the Civil Code.' Perhaps I would be among those who should gladly reverse the order of these terms and say 'Beyond the Civil Code but through it.'"

place below the level of the statute; and showed that at every stage of the legal process there is and must be creative activity.

5.   *He managed to resolve the traditional antinomy between the stable legal order and the everchanging social life and bring out the fact that legal rules must be simple summaries of sociological observation without losing their formal normative character.*

6.   *With his positive nature of things ... the supreme principle of justice and social utility as applied to a specific society, Gény created the third and last source of law [in addition to customary and legislative law] ... to be derived objectively from all the social [and behavioral] sciences which inform the judge or counsel of the actual state of the society and its needs."*

In his "Conclusion" to his monumental work, François Gény wrote the following about items 5 and 6 above: *"[183] ... Law, even in its positive form, appears to be a complex of rules which originate in the nature of things and should be derived through a more or less free interpretation from social elements which they have the purpose of ordering toward the common benefit. Law is inspired by justice and social usefulness; hence its essence places it above the formal sources which are its empirical revelations designated to direct human judgment more precisely, but which in themselves are always incomplete and imperfect ... The whole social research should play a role in the work of legal interpretation, on the sole condition that the value of each element will be recognized and they will be properly hierarchically classified. On the other hand, it would be in vain to try to enclose all the decisions required in practical life into a precise system of theorems, dominated by pure logic. While we seek the necessary precision, we must not forget that the very nature of the problem will always leave a place for subjective appreciation of the interpreter. It suffices that this discretion remains within certain limits and that it be guided by superior factors taken from the objective order ... [184] I only demand that, first, all the consequences be openly accepted, instead of remaining confined by the blind cult of statutory texts and logical conceptions; and, second, that we take into account the modern trends and the contemporary state of our culture, and recognize the place which belongs to social sciences in the practical legal method ... [185] Positive law must above all remain live. To live is to move and change. In the case of law it is even more: it is to struggle toward a constant and perfect adaptation to the exigencies of society ... Our conclusion tends to confirm that the purely formal and logical elements, available to the lawyers in the form of the external apparatus of positive law, are insufficient to satisfy the desiderata of law in action. The inevitable consequence is that the judicial process must look for the means needed to fulfill its mission outside of, and beyond, these elements. This is the essential principle of my thesis which it will be necessary to reject and destroy if one wants to positively contradict my ideas....*"[173]

The "insufficiency of the purely formal and logical elements" of the interpretation of positive law is remedied by the existence of additional or "extrinsic" methods of reasoning grounded in the "reason or purpose" of the law in general, general principles, such as "fairness," "social justice," and "unjust enrichment" that one can induce from a statute or a code article, or rather, a combination of statutes or code articles. These extrinsic methods of reasoning instill a new "blood" and, thus, a "new life" in the existing positive law to make that law the foundation for legal solutions and answers to be given to circumstances and situations which were not or could not have been contemplated to fall within the realm of application of the positive law the legislator had enacted on the basis of the then existing circumstances and situations. The positive law of "yesterday" is thereby kept alive by resorting to methods of interpretation based on "reason," on "principles" which are infinite in their nature and thus, fertile in application.

These "extrinsic" methods of reasoning to interpret positive law are perfect illustrations of this statement by Roscoe Pound that *"[t]he civilian is at his best in interpreting, developing and applying written texts ... In contrast, the common law lawyer is at his worst when confronted with a legislative text ..."*[174] Furthermore, as Jean Carbonnier wrote, from a philosophical point of view: *"Interpretation is the intellectual form of disobedience."* We are also told by the same legal scholar that *"[s]ince one tends to relate closely law to theology, one is tempted to find a kinship between the interpretation of laws and the interpretation of religious texts. They are, it is said, in different ways, sacred texts, revealed, inspired, and these words are not without consequences ... All our methods of interpretation are grounded, basically, on the same conception: that law is "will," "human and reasonable will," which enables the interpreter always to find the law through his own will, since men always find a way to get along."*[175]

a. Reasoning *a pari ratione* or *a simili ratione*

In a few words, to reason **a pari ratione** is to call on the "same reason" to make an "analogy." Such a method of interpretation or reasoning **a pari ratione**, consists in saying that where a statutory provision or a code article ex-

---

173. See Gény supra note 171 at p.451–460.

174. Roscoe Pound L.L.D., "What is the common law?"in *The Future of the Common Law*, Harvard University Press 1937.

175. J. Carbonnier, *Droit civil*, 22nd éd., PUF, 1994, p.250–251 #158.

presses a rule of law based on a "reason" to provide a legal solution to a certain set of circumstances known as "A," then this same rule of law and "for the same reason" should apply to a set of circumstances identified as "B," which presents the same characteristics as those that led the legislator to lay down a rule of law for the set of circumstances "A." This same method of reasoning is more fully expressed by the Latin maxims "**Ubi eadem est legis ratio, ibi eadem est legis dispositio**" (Where there is the same reason for the law, there is the same application of this law) or "**Ubi eadem ratio, ibi idem jus (or 'eadem est lex')**" (Where there is the same reason to decide, there is the same rule) or "**Ubi eadem est decisionis ratio, ibi eadem est legis dispositio**" (Where there is the same reason to decide, there must be the same decision).

Of much interest and relevance are the following statements made by some of the Roman commentators whose writings make up the Digest of Justinian (see supra Part I). Book I Title III:

4. Celsus: "Laws are not established concerning matters which can only happen in a single instance."

5. "For laws ought to be adapted to events which frequently and readily occur, rather than to such as rarely happen."

12. Julianus: "All matters cannot be specifically included in the laws or decrees of the Senate; but where their sense is clear in any instance, he who has jurisdiction of the same can apply it to others that are similar, and in this way administer justice."

13. Ulpianus: "For, as Pedius says, whenever anything has been introduced by law there is a good opportunity for extending it by interpretation or certain construction to other matters, where the same principle is involved."

25. Modestinus: "No principle of law or indulgent construction of equity permits matters which have been introduced for the welfare of mankind to be interpreted so rigorously as to be productive of hardship to them."

32. Julianus: " In cases where there are no written laws, that should be observed which has been established by usage and custom, and if anything is lacking therein, then whatever is nearest to, and resulting from it should be observed ..."[176]

François Gény wrote the following on "analogy" as a method of reasoning:

"*The force of analogy seems to rest in reality on a profound natural instinct, which constitutes in this instance a true sociological element the application of which*

---

176. S.P.Scott, A.M., *Corpus Juris Civilis, The Civil Law*, AMS Press Inc., 1973.

supplements the logical nature of the formal rules of law. In the depth of our spirit we feel, in effect, something like a need for equality before law, as a consequence of which the same fact situations should involve the same legal sanctions. This feeling does not only require that a rule applied to one person should apply to another under the same conditions. It requires that the ruling in such a case must be applied, except for particular reasons to the contrary, to an analogous case, that is a case which is essentially identical with the first one. There remains the question as to what is an essential identity. To solve it, we must penetrate the logical nature of the legal rule and extract from among the conditions of its injunction the principle which forms the tie between the positively known decision and that which is to be determined. This principle justifies analogy … [That] legal rule, set and consolidated in what we properly call the spirit of the statute, [has] a true character of a legal principle enacted by the legislator in specific form, but carrying within itself a broader and more fruitful element which analogy is capable to implement … Only a principle so understood appears to us as the fundamental and permanent reason for the statute ("ratio juris") and can determine the applicability of analogy."[177]

Let us illustrate with some examples of civil code articles.

In the French Civil Code, the contract of "exchange" is governed by Articles 1702 to 1707. This last Article 1707 states: "*[a]ll the other rules pertaining to the contract of sale apply as well to the contract of exchange.*" Since there are only six articles on this contract of "exchange," the last article, Article 1707, instructs us to look at the "*rules pertaining to the contract of sale*" to fill the gaps in the articles on "exchange." Sale and Exchange are two "subject matters" which we must relate one to the other by a reasoning in **pari materia**. But when we turn to the subject matter of "special privileges," we find that Article 2332-4 grants a privilege to the vendor-seller for "*the unpaid price of movables if still in the possession of the debtor, whether he has bought on credit or not.*" Article 2324 defines a privilege as "*a right that the nature of a claim gives to a creditor to be preferred to the other creditors […]*" Privileges, therefore, are to be interpreted restrictively, narrowly, as exceptions since they derogate from the general principle stated in Article 2284 according to which "*whoever has bound himself personally must fulfill his commitment from all his movable or immovable property, present and future.*"

The same general principle and "exceptions" are the law of the Louisiana Civil Code. As stated in **La.Civ.C.Art.3184** and **3185**, "*Privileges,*" being "*lawful causes of preference,*" "*can be claimed only for those debts to which [the priv-*

---

177. See Gény supra note 171 at p.382–384 #165.

ilege] is expressly granted in this Code." Article 3217 gives a list of "special privileges on particular movables" and its paragraph 7 grants such a privilege for *"the price due on movable effects, if they are yet in the possession of the purchaser."*

In other words, both sets of code articles make no specific reference to any "privilege" on any movable that has been the object of a contract of exchange, as contrasted with a contract of sale. Yet some French commentators writing about the privilege of a seller of an "immovable" and calling upon an **a pari ratione** reasoning have written that the reason for granting a privilege to a vendor of an immovable who has not been paid his price is the same reason that should justify creating a privilege in a contract of exchange with payment of the balance.[178]

Chapter 5 of Title 7 of Book I of the Louisiana Civil Code bears the title "Of Parental Authority." Article 216, in this chapter, states that *"a child remains under the authority of his father and mother, he is bound to obey them in every thing which is not contrary to good morals and the laws."* Article 220 allows the *"[f]athers and mothers ... during their life, [to] delegate a part of their authority to teachers ... and others to whom they entrust their children for their education ..."* We now bring in Article 236 which states: *"Fathers and mothers may justify themselves in an action begun against them for assault and battery, if they acted in defense of the persons of their children."* One question to ask is based on a change of facts that we stipulate as follows: father and mother have had to be away for a short period of time and have asked "grand Pa and grand Ma," i.e., one set of grandparents, to take their place in the family home until they return. What if, during that short period of time, "grand Pa and grand Ma" have had to "act in defense of the persons of their grandchildren" and, in doing so, have caused injuries and suffering to a stranger who meant to hurt the children? Wouldn't it be sensible or "reasonable" to transpose the "reason" which is the foundation of the fact pattern briefly describe in Article 236 under "Parental Authority" into the "unwritten but much similar" fact pattern involving grandparents, a fact pattern which is rather common in our days, so as to allow the grandparents to "justify themselves in an action begun against them for assault and battery"? Can we go further and make use of the same "reason" in a fact pattern that would involve more distant relatives than the grandparents, uncles and aunts for example? What about a couple of close "friends" of the father and mother of the children? If under Article 220 *"fa-*

---

178. Aubry et Rau, *Cours de Droit Civil Français*, 5ème édition, Tome Troisième, 1900–1902, p.284 #263.

thers and mothers may … delegate a part of their authority to teachers.… and others for their education …" what about a father and a mother entrusting to friends the "lives" of the children? Where the "reason" for the law of Article 236 is the same as the reason for a new rule of law that should be applicable to grandparents, relatives and even close friends, that new rule of law should be the same as the rule laid down in Article 236: "**Ubi eadem ratio, ibi idem jus (lex)**"!

Article 939 of the Louisiana Civil Code lays down the rule of law that "a successor must exist at the death of the decedent." One reason can be found in Articles 934 and 935: "*Succession occurs at the death of a person*"; "*Immediately at the death of the decedent, universal successors acquire ownership of the estate and particular successors acquire ownership of the things bequeathed to them.*" As a result, upon "the death of the decedent" his estate is immediately acquired by an "existing successor." The patrimony of the decedent will have a "successor who immediately acquires ownership." Let us change somewhat the fact pattern and postulate that the only "successor" to the decedent is an unborn child, a child still in his mother's womb: Can the "unborn" become a "successor" immediately at the death of the decedent and become a universal successor under Article 935? The "reason" why we postulated this "new" set of facts is because under La. Civ. C. Art. 26: "*An unborn child shall be considered as a natural person for whatever relates to its interests from the moment of conception. If the child is born dead, it shall be considered never to have existed as a person, except for purposes of actions resulting from its wrongful death.*" Thus, assuming the child is "unborn" at the time of the decedent's death, is this unborn child a "*successor that exists at the death of the decedent*"? According to Article 26 the unborn is considered as a natural person from the moment of conception and according to Article 24 "*a natural person is a human being*" to which Article 27 adds that "*all natural persons enjoy general legal capacity to have rights and duties.*" So, are we in a position to state that the "reason" which is the justification for Article 939 exists just as well in the event the successor is "an unborn," yet a natural person? In the affirmative, then the rule of law expressed in this Article 939 should be the same as in the case of the unborn becoming a successor. Obviously, the rights and duties of the "unborn" will be exercised by "the father" who "*during the marriage is the administrator of the estate of his minor children and the mother in case of his interdiction or absence during said interdiction or absence […]*"[179] Furthermore, "*parents have during marriage the enjoyment of the property of their children until their majority or*

---

179. La. Civ. C. art. 221.

emancipation[…]"[180] The maxim "**ubi eadem est legis ratio, ibi eadem est legis dispositio**" does find room for application in this "unprovided for set of circumstances."

Let us take one example from Book 2 of the Louisiana Civil Code entitled "*Things and the Different Modifications of Ownership.*" The Code article we have selected is Article 784. It states: "*A boundary is the line of separation between contiguous lands. A boundary marker is a natural or artificial object that marks on the ground the line of separation of contiguous lands.*" Considering that there exist many bodies of water in the State of Louisiana, can we substitute "contiguous bodies of water" to "contiguous lands" and still apply the rule of law laid down in Article 786, for example? This article states: "*The boundary may be fixed upon the demand of an owner or of one who possesses as owner […]*" The reason for this article is quite simply to allow an owner to properly identify his property to make use of it as he sees fit without intruding on the same right of the owner of a contiguous tract of land. We could possibly use an **in pari materia** reasoning, as discussed above, and simply say that the "matter" of land can easily be replaced by the "matter" of water as both can be owned as private things under La. Civ. C. Art. 453. On the other hand, one could counter such an **in pari materia** reasoning with an **a contrario sensu** or an **inclusio unius exclusio alterius** reasoning and say that in using the words "contiguous lands" the legislator meant what it wrote and that if it had intended to include "bodies of water" it would have said so in the text of the article.

When one makes an argument **a pari ratione**, one goes far beyond the literal meaning of words to circumvent, as in this case, a likely argument **a contrario sensu**. Indeed, relying on the **ratio legis** or "reason for a statute or code article" allows for a broad and more encompassing argument unhindered by merely logical arguments of semantics, grammar, or terminology. As Portalis had advised a reader of a civil code to do: "search for the spirit (and we could add: the soul) of the law where the letter kills." So, in the instance where we would have two or more owners of one and the same body of water, why not allow an owner to mark the line of separation between his private property in that body of water when it happens to be contiguous with the private property of another owner over that same body of water? Why couldn't "artificial objects" consisting in "mooring buoys" or "anchor buoys" or "posts" or "poles" be considered as the "boundary markers" of an owner's property lines?

---

180. La. Civ. C. art. 223.

b. Reasoning *a fortiori ratione: a minori ad majus; a majori ad minus*

Like the previous method of reasoning, this particular method of reasoning is also grounded on the "ratio," or "reason," that justifies and explains why a statute or a code article is written in the words apparently intentionally chosen by the legislature. However, instead of making a reasoning **a pari**, or, one could say, an horizontal reasoning suggested by "an equivalent, identical reason," as illustrated above, when one reasons a fortiori one is making, a vertical reasoning. Such a vertical reasoning is suggested by the word "**fortiori**," which comes from the Latin "**fortis**," meaning "strong, powerful."

The Oxford English Dictionary gives the following definition: "**a fortiori, a. from, fortiori-stronger.** *With stronger reason, still more conclusively.*"[181] Black's Law Dictionary gives the following definition: "*a fortiori, adv. [Latin]. By even greater force of logic; even more so it follows <if a 14-year-old child cannot sign a binding contract, then, a fortiori, a 13-year-old cannot>.*"[182] In the *Dictionary of the Civil Code*, we find the following description: "*A fortiori. Accepted Lat. expression, short for* **a fortiori causa** *(or* **ratione***), meaning 'for a more forceful reason,' or 'even more so.'*" And under the word "**argument**," we find: "*argument a fortiori. Reasoning consisting in applying the rule given in a text to a case not contemplated by that text, because a reference to the 'reason' behind the rule (**ratio legis**) makes it obvious that that rule offers even greater reasons to apply to the case not expressly contemplated by the text. Ex. Qui peut le plus peut le moins; Whoever can the most, can the least.*"[183]

Let us return, here, to the example given above in Black's Law Dictionary: "if a 14 year cannot ... then '*a fortiori*' a 13 year cannot." One can label this form of reasoning **a fortiori ratione**, as going "from the lesser to the greater," or a **minori ad majus**. Indeed, the reason why a 14-year-old cannot sign a contract is because of his lack of understanding, lack of maturity, which lack of understanding or maturity is found "even more so" in a 13-year-old; therefore, for an ever greater reason, a 13-year-old should not be allowed to sign a contract.

A reasoning **a fortiori ratione a minori ad majus** can be made on Article 2897 of the La. Civ. C. This article reads as follows: "*When the thing lent is damaged by a fortuitous event from which the borrower could have protected the thing lent by using a thing of his own or, when being unable to preserve both things, the borrower chose to preserve a thing of his own, he is liable for the dam-*

---

181. 2nd ed. Clarendon Press-Oxford, 1989.
182. *Black's Law Dictionary*, 10th ed., Thomson Reuters, 2009, 2014.
183. *Dictionary of the Civil Code*, LexisNexis, 2014.

age to the thing lent." What to do if instead of *"the thing lent being <u>damaged</u> by a fortuitous event,"* the fortuitous event had *"<u>destroyed</u>"* the thing lent? Wouldn't it be easy for the court presented with this issue to "reason a **fortiori ratione from the lesser, a minori** (damaged) **to the greater ad majus** (destroyed)" and apply the law of the same Article 2897 and hold the borrower "liable for the damage to the thing lent"?

La. Civ. C. Articles 389 and 390 provide, in one instance, that a court may place a natural person of the age of majority under an order either of full or limited interdiction when, because of an infirmity, that person cannot take care of herself or her property. Although the "wording" of these articles focuses on the person's own care or own property, one may ask what can be the "reason" behind the court's order? If such a person can neither take care of herself nor of her property for the reason that her "infirmity" makes it impossible for her to take care of herself and her property, shouldn't that same person be prevented from "taking care of another" not only for the same reason (**a pari ratione**) but for an even more powerful reason, **a fortiori ratione a minori** (the person herself) **ad majus** (another person)?

The maxim given in the *Dictionary of the Civil Code* is of the same nature in the sense that it concerns reasoning **a fortiori ratione**. However, it describes this form of reasoning in a positive manner when it says that one who can do the most can, obviously, do the least. This form of reasoning a fortiori would be labelled "from the greater to the lesser" or **a majori ad minus** or, still, from the more important to the less important. For example: if I can enter into an authentic juridical act which "is a writing executed before a notary public or other officer authorized to perform that function, in the presence of two witnesses, and signed by each party who executed it, by each witness, and by each notary public before whom it was executed" (La. Civ. C. Art 1833(A)), **a fortiori ratione a majori ad minus** can I enter into *"an act under private signature [which] need not be written by the parties, but must be signed by them."* (La. Civ. C. Art. 1837). Entering into an act under private signature is a much easier thing to do than entering into an authentic act for the reason that the interests of the parties involved in an authentic act as well as the rights of third parties must be fully protected by all the formalities required. When the juridical act contemplated is of lesser importance and less susceptible of having detrimental effects on third parties, it is not as important to require formalities. So, one who can do the most in the form of an authentic act can do the least by entering into an act under private signature.

La. Civ. C. Art. 3473 provides a very good "legal" illustration of such a reasoning from the greater to the lesser. It states: *"Ownership and other real rights in immovables may be acquired by the prescription of ten years.*" The ownership of an immovable is the most important real right a person can have over an immovable, or any "thing" for that matter: "*A. Ownership is the right that confers on a person direct, immediate, and exclusive authority over a thing. The owner of a thing may use, enjoy, and dispose of it within the limits and under the conditions established by law.*" (Art. 477). It is obvious, reasoning a fortiori ratione, from the greater to the lesser, that if the most important real right, the right of ownership (the greater), can be acquired by prescription in ten years, some real rights of lesser importance (the lesser), should be able to be acquired also by prescription. And, indeed, La. Civ. C. Article 740 states that "[a]pparent servitudes may be acquired by title, by destination of the owner, or by acquisitive prescription."

Now that these many different methods or kinds of reasoning and interpretation have been explained and illustrated with the help of Code articles, it is time to turn to the jurisprudence and look at some cases to find out if and how the Louisiana courts make use of these methods of reasoning under "concrete and empirical" circumstances.

Chapter 3

Methods of Reasoning
and the Courts

The "jurisprudence," as a concept that, at civil law, encompasses the decisions of the courts, is, one the one hand, a "secondary" source of law[184] and, on the other hand, "the true expression of the civil law."[185] To illustrate these two features of the "jurisprudence" we will now place them in the context of three decisions of the Louisiana Supreme Court. To that effect, we will consider these three decisions with one specific goal in mind, which will be to attempt to identify "if," "where," and "how" in these three decisions, the methods of reasoning described above have contributed to the Court's legal analysis of the issues raised in these cases and, ultimately, in the rulings the Court handed down. These three decisions have been selected, after much deliberation, out of a broad choice of interesting decisions, because we came to the conclusion that, all together, they illustrate clearly and in different ways the use by the Louisiana Supreme Court of all the existing methods of interpretation and reasoning. These three decisions stand as examples, if not models, of a well-crafted legal reasoning, logical, methodical, quasi "mathematical" in its reading of articles of the Louisiana Civil Code against the background of the facts the Supreme Court had to work with.

It is obviously not the duty of a Court to identify, in advance and by name, which method of reasoning it is about to use in this holding or that holding all through its opinion. Such is more the responsibility of an outsider, be it a legal scholar—commentator or a case—note writer interested in penetrating

---

184. See above Part I, "The Making of a Civil Code"; see also Portalis's speech in *Code Napoléon or Code Portalis*, Alain Levasseur, XLIII Tul. L. Rev., 1969, p.762–774.

185. A. Esmein, *Case Law and Doctrine,* translation by Shael Herman, 18 Loy. L. Rev. 23–27 (1971–72).

the thinking process, whether inductive or deductive, that could have led the judges to write an opinion, be it unanimous or majority.

The exercise we are about to embark on is aimed at attempting to provide a technical look, ours obviously here, from the inside of an opinion. It is not at all meant to bear any judgment on the legal substance and value of that opinion. In other words, we are not writing a case-note with the intent to support or to criticize the court in its opinion. The opinion "is" what it is and we will merely and artificially dissect it in segments with one exclusively practical purpose in mind: illustrate the use by the court of the methods of reasoning in each segment we have singled out. Borrowing from the prior section above on the listing and description of the "Methods of Reasoning," the reader should then be in a position to decide whether he would have used the same methods of reasoning that we will have identified as being the court's methods of reasoning. In this exercise, the reader is invited to "juggle," wisely and rationally, with the methods of reasoning discussed and illustrated above. Indeed, to one method of reasoning there is a counter method of reasoning so that, when these methods of reasoning are combined or pitted against each other, the reader will be in a position to elaborate his own personal "concurring" or "dissenting" opinion!

As regards the three cases below, we will give, first, a brief statement of the facts of each case before proceeding, step by step, through the court's legal analysis for the purpose of identifying and naming the methods of reasoning that the Court appears to have used even though the Court did not announce in advance what method of reasoning it was going to use here and there.

Neila Leblanc, wife Eugene James LOYACANO

v.

Eugene James LOYACANO

Supreme Court of Louisiana[186]

Facts [from the Opinion]:

In 1971 Mrs. Neila LeBlanc Loyacano was granted a divorce from her husband, Dr. Eugene Loyacano, on the grounds of living separate and apart for two years pursuant to Louisiana Revised Statute 9:301. The default divorce judgment provided Mrs. Loyacano with $1,000 per month alimony and $1,000 per month for the support of their two minor children. Dr. Loyacano voluntarily supplemented these payments with extra sums which were discontinued upon his remarriage in February of 1974.

---

186. 358 So. 2d 304 (1978).

Mrs. Loyacano filed a rule to increase both the alimony and child support awards in May of 1974. Following an involved procedural history, during which Dr. Loyacano filed rules to reduce the child support award and reduce or revoke the alimony, hearings were held on the respective rules in October of 1975. Child support was awarded in the amount of $500 per month per child and the alimony was reduced to $300 per month. Both parties appealed to the court of appeal. The child support award was affirmed but the $300 per month alimony award was revoked.[187] We granted Mrs. Loyacano's application for certiorari to review the judgment revoking alimony.[188]

I. Opinion on First Hearing: Dennis, Justice

A.   Alimony after divorce is governed by Article 160 of the Civil Code which authorizes a court, under proper circumstances, to allow the wife alimony out of the property and earnings of the husband. There is no provision of positive law which expressly authorizes a court to grant alimony after divorce to the husband. Defendant-respondent contends that Article 160, therefore, is an unconstitutional denial of equal protection of law prohibited by both the Fourteenth Amendment to the United States Constitution and Article I, s.3 of the Louisiana Constitution of 1974.

Comment: *the Court, as "interpreter" of the primary sources of law applicable in a case, begins with a listing of those primary sources of law which will control in this case. These sources are: the Constitution(s); the Louisiana Civil Code.*[189]

B.   The argument based on federal constitutional grounds may have merit. We do not consider it here, however, for we agree that to allow only wives to collect alimony after divorce would amount at least to arbitrary and unreasonable discrimination against persons because of sex and thus a denial of equal protection under the Louisiana Constitution. Although not based solely on sex, such classifications for purposes of entitlement to alimony after divorce probably were founded on the assumption that all former husbands have sufficient means for their support, or that few divorced women have property and earnings out of which alimony could be paid, or upon both. If these propositions were ever true, common experience tells us that the deviations from them are now too numerous for the classifications to withstand equal protection challenge.

---

187. Loyacano v. Loyacano, 343 So.2d 365 (La.App. 4th Cir. 1977).

188. 345 So.2d 57 (La.1977).

189. See Lamonica supra note 145: "*A fundamental tenet of a system predicated upon a civil law tradition is that the legislature—not the judiciary—is the governmental body elected by its constituents to enact for them the authoritative allocation of values through law.*"

Comment: *looking back in time, the Court makes a first attempt at finding the "reason" which might explain and justify the "written law" the Court is given to interpret and apply.*

C.   The failure of the legislature to expressly authorize the allowance of alimony after divorce for male citizens, however, does not necessarily invalidate Civil Code article 160. Because Louisiana is a civil law jurisdiction, the absence of express law does not imply a lack of authority for courts to provide relief. In all civil matters, where positive law is silent, the judge is bound by the Civil Code to proceed and decide according to equity, i.e., according to natural law and reason, or to received usages. La.C.C. art. 21. This Court has recognized its duty to proceed and decide important issues under these circumstances on many occasions.

Comment: *these statements embody the essence of the relationship, which exists in the civil law, between the legislature and the Courts. We have emphasized and illustrated this relationship in many of the writings given in the first part of this book. As the Court purposefully states: "Because Louisiana is a civil law jurisdiction the absence of express law does not imply a lack of authority for courts to provide relief ..."*

D.   In order to ascertain if there truly is no positive law either authorizing or prohibiting the allowance of alimony for divorced men we must carefully examine the legislative expressions in the light of the other articles of the Civil Code pertaining to the application and construction of laws. We are also mindful of the doctrine of reputable scholars, which teaches that civilian judges are not required to depend merely upon a logical analysis of the existing statutes, but may employ other recognized methods of interpretation. They may perform extensive exegesis to discover the original legislative intent; legislative texts may be interpreted so as to give them an application that is consistent with the contemporary conditions they are called upon to regulate; and a particular conflict of interests before the court may be resolved in accordance with the general policy considerations which induced legislative action rather than by reliance on logical deductions from the language of the text.

Comment: *1) As a logical follow up on the above, the Court, mindful of the role of judges in a civil law jurisdiction, will call upon "recognized methods of interpretation," which will take the Court far beyond a mere "logical analysis." Notice that "reputable scholars" are now added as a persuasive source of law in addition to the articles of the Civil Code, which are a primary source of law in this case. 2) Particularly important to the developments to come in this opinion, are the words: "general policy considerations which induced legislative action rather ... logical deductions from the language of the text."*

E.   Both the codal and the doctrinal principles should be employed to discover the meaning of the words of the law.

Comment: *of particular relevance here is the Court's reference to "principles," both codal and doctrinal, to go beyond the words of the written law. This short statement illustrates perfectly the triangle of the sources of law at civil law*:

Law

Courts   Doctrine

F.   The general policy consideration and practical reason which appear to have induced the legislature to provide alimony after divorce was to prevent divorced women without sufficient means from becoming wards of the state. Although the legislative history of Civil Code article 160 sheds little light on the different treatment accorded husbands and wives, the most reasonable and probable basis is the assumption that married men were capable of supporting dependents, whereas married women usually could not support themselves. Although the assumption may have had substantial empirical support at the time of the legislation's enactment, it is clearly outmoded in today's society in which nearly half of the married women are employed and contribute to the standard of living of their families. The evolving nature of the role played by women in our state was clearly and emphatically recognized by the provision banning invidious gender based discrimination in the Louisiana Constitution of 1974. Indeed, the debates at the 1973 Louisiana Constitutional Convention concerning the provision reflect that the delegates considered alimony to be an important statutory right and contemplated that the new equal protection clause would require that it be granted equally to both sexes.

Comment: *1) Notice the contrast and its implications between "general policy" and "practical reason." Possibly a warning that in its legal analysis the Court will make more use of methods of interpretation based on "reason" than of methods based on words. "Reason" will probably span a large swath of time, likely decades. 2) In the sentence "[a]lthough the assumption may have had substantial empirical support at the time of the legislation's enactment, it is clearly outmoded in today's society in which nearly half of the married women are employed and contribute to the standard of living of their families." Here the Court gives us a hint that a reasoning* **a pari ratione** *will play a major role. In other words, at one time men were employed and contributed to the standard of living of their families, now women are employed and, in turn, contribute to the standard of living of their families just as much as men do or did. Thus the reason which explained and justified the obligation of men/husbands to pay alimony to their wives, is the same reason today that can easily explain and justify that a woman should pay alimony to her (former) husband when the latter is in need. 3) In the fol-*

*lowing two sentences, the Court could be said to make both an **in pari materia**
and a **pro subjecta materia** reasoning (**in pari materia**: roles of men and women
in our state; **pro subjecta materia**: the increasing and expanding nature of women's
activities and responsibilities).*

G.   Consequently, when we attribute to Article 160 the meaning that a
present day legislator would have attributed to it, we must assume that he
would have taken cognizance of the increasing and expanding nature of
women's activities and responsibilities, as well as our constitution's prohibition of arbitrary or unreasonable gender based legal classifications, and that
he would not have intended by the legislation to discriminate against husbands
who have not sufficient means for their maintenance by declaring them inel-
igible for alimony after a divorce.

Comment: *1) This is a reasoning **a pari ratione** to explain how the reason
which justifies the law of Article 160 as written could not possibly discriminate.
Furthermore, the Constitution prohibits discrimination; thus, a present day legislature would rely on the "same reason" if it were asked to adopt a statute "for
the benefit of men" after divorce. 2) One can also see here a **teleological interpretation** of Article 160 in the sense that the Court considers the rule of Article
160 "must be applied in such a way as to fulfill its end, its purpose and, thus, must
be interpreted in light of its purpose."*[190]

H.   Accordingly, the question of alimony for a husband after divorce is a
civil matter upon which there is no express or implied law, and we are bound
to proceed and decide according to equity. La.C.C. art. 21. Our appeal to natural law and reason informs us that the general policy considerations which
induced the legislature to authorize alimony allowances for wives after divorce
would also be served by granting such support to either spouse when the circumstances provided by Article 160 prevail. Equity and our constitution demand that the husband be awarded alimony under the same circumstances in
which it can be claimed by the wife. For these reasons, we conclude that a
Louisiana court may allow alimony to a husband after divorce, under the same
circumstances in which it can be claimed by the wife, and that the contention
of the defendant-respondent that Civil Code Article 160 denies equal protection of the law is without merit.

Comment: *1) The fact that "[t]here is no express or implied law" is not the
end of the judge's investigation in a civil law jurisdiction because "the absence of
express law does not imply a lack of authority for courts to provide relief." (See*

---

190. See *Dictionary of the Civil Code*, LexisNexis, 2014; word: **téléologique**.

*this case supra). La. Civ. C. Art. 21, now Art. 4, empowers the Court "to proceed according to equity." This same Art. 21 or 4 instructs the Court to "resort to justice, reason." Therefore, all methods of reasoning based on "reason" find their grounding, their **raison d'être** in Art. 21, or Art. 4, in the Civil Code today. Likewise, the methods of reasoning based on the meaning of words find their grounding and raison d'être in La. C. C. arts. 9 to 12. 2) In this excerpt, the Court makes, again, a reasoning **a pari ratione** (which stresses the strength of such a method of reasoning) in stating that "the husband be awarded alimony under the same circumstances in which it can be claimed by the wife."*

The extremely unusual set of circumstances involved in this case and the challenge it presented to the Supreme Court were enriched by two other opinions, a concurring one and a dissenting one.

Marcus, Justice (concurring)

[Actually, Justice Marcus concurred in the result that was not of much legal importance, but his opinion did not go along with the majority opinion on its choice of methods of reasoning.]

I.   I consider that there are many good reasons to support alimony to a wife after divorce; therefore, La. Civil Code art. 160 provides a reasonable legislative classification, not arbitrary, and rests upon a ground of difference having a fair and substantial relation to the object of the legislation, so that all persons similarly situated are treated alike.

<u>Comment</u>: *where Justice Marcus states that "there are many good reasons to support alimony to a wife after divorce," one could identify his method of reasoning as "**ratione legis stricta**" (good reasons to support alimony to a wife), as well as a hint of reasoning **a contrario sensu** (what is said about a "wife" is not said about a "husband"). Furthermore, "all persons similarly situated are treated alike," means that all wives similarly situated and all husbands similarly situated are to be treated alike.*

J.   Moreover, I disagree with the majority that courts are permitted to allow alimony to a husband after divorce where the legislature has expressly allowed alimony after divorce only to a wife under conditions set forth in La. Civil Code art. 160. I consider the majority opinion in this respect amounts to legislation by the court.

<u>Comment</u>: *Justice Marcus in his reasoning both **a contrario sensu** and **ratione legis stricta** likely relied on then La. Civ. C. Art. 13 (now Art. 9): "When a law is clear and unambiguous and its application does not lead to absurd consequences, the law shall be applied as written and no further interpretation may be made in search of the intent of the legislature."*

Sanders, Chief Justice (dissenting)

K.   Perhaps, the most obvious error in the judgment here is the postulation that the law is silent as to whether or not a husband is entitled to alimony after divorce. Article 160 of the Louisiana Civil Code authorizes alimony, but limits it to "the wife (who) has not been at fault." The article further requires that the wife be without "sufficient means for her support." The alimony is payable from the "property and earnings of the husband" but cannot exceed one-third of his income. The language of the article clearly excludes a husband's entitlement to alimony from the wife.

Comment: *since the law, i.e., Art.160, is not silent it must be read and interpreted as is because the law "is clear and free from all ambiguity ..." (La. Civ. C. Art. 13 at the time). Thus, Chief Justice Sanders was following a **reasoning ratio legis stricta** and a **contrario sensu** (expressio unius, exclusio alterius — Qui dicit de uno, de altero negat).*

L.   This exclusion is reinforced by the history of the article. Article 301 of the Code Napoléon (1804) allowed either husband or wife in necessitous circumstances to receive alimony if he or she had obtained a divorce. This provision was omitted in the Louisiana Civil Code of 1808, where divorce, as distinguished from separation from bed and board, was not recognized. Although divorce was authorized in the Louisiana Civil Code of 1825, the provision for alimony after divorce was intentionally omitted. Thus, no alimony was payable, since alimony after divorce is in the nature of a pension and must be specifically authorized.

Comment: *this is a method of reasoning consisting of looking at the history of the Code articles, particularly at its historical sources such as the Code Napoléon and the Louisiana Civil Codes of 1808 and 1825. We can identify also a reasoning **pro subjecta materia** (the subject matters being: divorce, separation from bed and board, husband and wife financial situations).*

M.   The history of the statute demonstrates the intentional legislative restriction of alimony-after-divorce to the wife. Hence, resort to equity under Article 21 of the Louisiana Civil Code is unjustified.

Comment: *this is reasoning on the basis of the **preparatory works** and the history of the statute of 1827. On the basis of that history, Chief Justice Sanders concludes that a reasoning **ratione legis stricta** is the logical outcome. Thus, there is no "reason" to go beyond the statute and Art.160 of the La. C.C. Furthermore, one cannot call upon the "equity" of Art. 21 (now Art. 4) to find whatever other reason is not there. For Justice Marcus and Chief Justice Sanders the strict single reason behind La. C.C. Art. 160, i.e. the separate classification of wives for al-*

imony purposes, establishes a fair and substantial relationship to the object of the legislation.

ON REHEARING

SANDERS, Chief Justice.

N.   Does LSA-C.C. Art. 160 allow alimony to a needy husband?

The very first article of the Civil Code provides that "(l)aw is a solemn expression of legislative will." Article 2 discusses the attributes of the law, stating: "(i)t orders and permits and forbids, it announces rewards and punishments, its provisions generally relate not to solitary or singular cases, but to what passes in the ordinary course of affairs." "When a law is clear and free from all ambiguity, the letter of it is not to be disregarded, under the pretext of pursuing its spirit." LSA-C.C. Art. 13.

Comment: *we have, here, an exemplary civilian approach to identifying a legal issue so as to call on the appropriate and relevant primary sources of law. The issue at stake, the matter to be addressed, is one of "interpretation." The controlling primary sources of law are, therefore, La. C.C. Articles 1, 2, 13 et seq. This opinion on rehearing is then built on these Code articles and the methods of reasoning they command.*

O.   The language of Article 160 clearly excludes a husband's entitlement to alimony from his wife. It limits alimony to "the wife" payable from the "property and earnings of the husband." This exclusion is reinforced by the history of the article. Article 301 of the Code Napoléon (1804) allowed either husband or wife in necessitous circumstances to receive alimony if he or she had obtained a divorce. This provision was omitted from the Louisiana Civil Code of 1808, where divorce, as distinguished from separation from bed and board, was not recognized. Although divorce was authorized in the Louisiana Civil Code of 1825, the provision for alimony after divorce was intentionally omitted. Thus, no alimony was payable, since alimony after divorce is in the nature of a pension and must be specifically authorized.

On March 19, 1827, the Legislature in "An Act Relative to Divorces" provided for alimony after divorce for the first time. The alimony was limited to "the wife who has obtained the divorce" and payable "out of the property of her husband." The identical provision was later reenacted in Act 307 of 1855. The provision was later incorporated in the Louisiana Civil Code of 1870 as Article 160. See C. E. Lazarus, "What Price Alimony," 11 La.L.Rev. 401, 412–415. The history of the article demonstrates the deliberate legislative restriction of alimony-after-divorce to the wife.

Article 160 speaks clearly on the subject of alimony. It limits alimony to needy wives.

Comment: *on rehearing, Chief Justice Sanders is resorting to the same methods of reasoning that he and Justice Marcus had used in their concurring-dissenting opinions on first hearing. As stated in the comment immediately above, these methods of reasoning are based on the Code articles on "The Application and Construction of Laws," as applied to Article 160. In addition the Opinion resorts to a reasoning* **ratione legis stricta** *and a* **reasoning a contrario sensu,** *as the two Justices had done in their concurring and dissenting opinions on first hearing.*

In conclusion, and for constitutional law reasons to a large extent, the Justices appeared to have agreed on the opinions that this matter very much recommends itself for legislative action and that the Court would not want to usurp the legislative function and responsibility by grafting onto our law a constitutionally permissible alimony provision.

Theodore L. Tannehill, Jr.

v.

Estelle Scott Southerland Tannehill et al.

Estelle Scott Tannehill

v.

Theodore L. Tannehill, Jr.

Supreme Court of Louisiana[191]

Facts [from the Opinion]:

In these consolidated actions, Theodore L. Tannehill, Jr. seeks to establish judicially that he is not the father of Scott, the child born to Estelle Scott Southerland Tannehill. One of the suits is an action en desaveu. The child was born during the existence of a marriage between Theodore and Estelle. [He] contends that the child is not his because of childhood diseases, which resulted in his sterility. Tannehill's allegations in the action en desaveu are that he contracted mumps at the age of twelve 'which was further complicated with encephalitis,' which resulted in an 'impediment to the natural maturity of petitioner's reproductive system,' and that he was 'unable physically and biologically to produce spermatozoa.' The district court sustained an exception of no cause of action, and would not allow any proof of sterility on the trial of the consolidated cases. The first time this case reached the Court of Appeal, it

---

191. 261 La. 933 (1972); 261 So. 2d 619.

affirmed the district court's sustaining of the exception of no cause of action to the disavowal action. Only two cases in Louisiana have been located in which a disavowal of paternity has been allowed: Kaufman v. Kaufman, La.App., 146 So.2d 199 and Singley v, Singley, La.App., 140 So.2d 546. In both cases, the child involved was born more than three hundred days after a judgment of separation had been rendered.

I. Opinion
DIXON, Justice

A.   The Louisiana Supreme Court has never allowed a disavowal of paternity. From the results of numerous attacks on the paternity of children through the years (see Cavanaugh, 'Action En Desaveu,' 23 L. Law Rev. 759), it is apparent that the presumption of paternity in Louisiana has been rigorously applied. Article 184 of the Civil Code: "The law considers the husband of the mother as the father of all children conceived during the marriage."

Comment: *notice that the Supreme Court starts its approach to solving the legal issue raised in this case by putting forward its own jurisprudence first before any statutory law, like Civil Code articles. It states forcefully that "[t]he Louisiana Supreme Court has never allowed a disavowal of paternity," despite the many "attacks on the paternity of children through the years." The Court justifies its position on the basis of a "presumption" that "has been rigorously applied" by the courts. This presumption resides in Article 184 of the Civil Code. A proper civil law approach, in a civilian jurisdiction, would have quoted Civil Code Article 184 first before referring to the Courts' application of that Article. It is obvious that the Civil Code Article preceded in time, and in ranking among the sources of law, any possible interpretation by a court. Giving the Supreme Court first "ranking" is, to a "civilian," somewhat of a warning sign that whatever the Supreme Court has done in the past is not about to be modified, or even less overruled, without the same Court being presented with an extremely convincing argument to the contrary. Justice Barham will attempt to do this without much success.*

B.   Disavowal is prohibited when based on the 'natural impotence' of the father. C.C. 185. Disavowal is prohibited when sought because of the adultery of the wife unless the birth of the child has been concealed from the father. C.C. 185; but see Trahan v. Trahan, La. App., 142 So.2d 571. Even in cases when the child is born prior to the one hundred eightieth day of marriage, disavowal is prohibited if the husband of the mother was acquainted with the circumstances of the pregnancy at the time of the marriage, or acknowledged the child at the registry of the birth or the baptism. C.C. 190. In all cases, even where the presumption of paternity ceases, the father is prohibited from disavowing his child unless he brings the action within a month of the birth or within two months after his return to the place of birth, or after the discovery of the fraudulent concealment. C.C. 191.

In spite of the presumption of paternity, the father is allowed to disavow the child when the mother has been guilty of adultery and the birth has been concealed from him. C.C. 185; but see Trahan v. Trahan, supra.

The presumption of paternity does not exist when the child is born before the one hundred eightieth day of the marriage, and does not exist with respect to children born more than three hundred days after the dissolution of the marriage or after judgment of separation. C.C. 186, 187.

Nor does the presumption of paternity exist when the husband has been so remote from the wife that cohabitation has been physically impossible.

  Comment: *since the strength of the presumption of paternity and, **a contrario**, the impossibility of an action in disavowal are based on the same reason which is to protect the child and assure him that he will have a father, exceptions to that presumption must be kept to a minimum [**exceptiones sunt strictissimae interpretationis**—exceptions must be interpreted very narrowly]. Actually, the only exception to the presumption of paternity of the husband-father applies when the wife-mother has been guilty of adultery and the birth of the child concealed from her husband. (La.C.C.185).*

C.   The codal provisions prevent the disavowal of paternity except within extremely narrow limits, and then only if done promptly after the birth. The policy of the State, as found in the statutes and as perpetuated in the jurisprudence, has been to protect innocent children against attacks upon their paternity. Williams v. Williams, 230 La. 1, 87 So.2d 707.

  Comment: *in this short paragraph one could say that the Supreme Court is reasoning, as above, according to the maxim "**exceptiones sunt strictissimae interpretationis.**" The Court is also referring to the "policy of the State as found in the statutes" as being the "**ratio juris**" (policy of the State) and the **ratio legis** (as found in the statutes) for keeping any exception to the principle to only one exception admissible under one code article. The broad notion of "**ratio juris**" is found in the narrower and particular "**ratio legis**" of each statute (lex). That "**ratio legis**" has for its purpose "to protect innocent children against attacks upon their paternity."*

D.   The father's argument is that the prohibition against disavowal on account of impotence of the husband does not prevent disavowal on account of the sterility of the husband, because: impotence and sterility are two different and well defined conditions; that it is possible for an impotent husband to conceive, but not scientifically possible for conception to result from the union of a woman with a 'sterile' man.

Comment: *the father's argument is built on the method of reasoning that states, "to include one is to exclude the other—inclusio unius, exclusio alterius." Where the Civil Code prohibits a disavowal "on account of impotence" it "does not prevent disavowal on account of the sterility of the husband." In addition, by drawing a distinction between "impotence" and "sterility," the father can be said to make the argument that one cannot reason "from the lesser to the greater," or "a fortiori a minori ad majus." Indeed, because impotence does not mean sterility, impotence is not a lesser form of sterility than sterility itself, since a sterile man cannot conceive whereas an impotent man could possibly conceive.*

E.   Neither proposition can be sustained without equivocation. We are in a poor position to determine with precision what was understood by the French at the beginning of the 19th century by the term l'impuissance. The French made a distinction between 'natural impotence' and 'impotence due to an accident.' Exactly what was meant by accidental impotence is not clear to us now, and was not clear to Planiol. (See 1 Planiol, Civil Law Treatise, Part 1, No. 1433 (La.L.Inst.Trans.)). In the English language, prior to the 19th century, one meaning of 'impotence' was 'wholly lacking in sexual power.' The New Century Dictionary of the English Language, Appleton-Century.

Human impotence is a problem as old as Western civilization. (See Genesis 17:17, "Then Abraham fell on his face and laughed, and said to himself, 'Shall a child be born to a man who is a hundred years old? Shall Sarah, who is ninety years old, bear a child?'").

However, until modern times, failure to procreate was 'generally accepted as a female responsibility, and in many parts of the world the possibility that a normally potent male might be infertile is still not considered.' 21 Encyclopedia Britannica, 397, 398. About 10% of the married population is involuntarily sterile, the causes for infertility divided about one-third to male factors, one-third to female and one-third to common difficulties.

We cannot say how much scientific knowledge was available to the French scholars at the time of the adoption of the Code Napoléon. It is not likely that they were aware of the microscopic isolation of spermatozoa. But if the French and Louisiana lawmakers understood 'l'impuissance' and 'impotence' to mean 'wholly lacking in sexual power,' as we think they must have, must we not conclude that they would also have forbidden disavowal for sterility of the male? The lawmakers did prohibit disavowal when the husband of the mother was unable to perform the sex act. Why, then, should we believe they would have permitted disavowal when the husband actually fulfilled the conjugal union by coitus? If we assume the 18th and 19th century lawmakers made a distinction between 'impotence' and male sterility, as the father now urges us to do, we must nevertheless conclude that the greater includes the lesser. For the ancients, 'impotence' was the greater disability. We can in no way attribute to the ancients even a suspicion that an impotent man was capable of procreation.

It has only been in the middle of the 20th century that enough data has been gathered to form a body of scientific knowledge concerning its nature. From the little that is now known, it is thought that impotence is not necessarily a constant condition in a male, and is not necessarily pathological in origin, but is a variable condition and often psychological in origin.

   Comment: *in this long paragraph the Court makes use of methods of reasoning based on: "preparatory works"; "comparative law"; "ab auctoritate"; "a fortiori ratione." 1) The Supreme Court makes some references to a variety of sources of "information" to help in properly describing the meaning of "words" such as: "impotence v. impuissance" and "natural v. accidental impotence." In this respect, the Court is reasoning "ab auctoritate" where it states: "[t]he French made"; citing "Planiol"; referring also to to the "New Century Dictionary of the English Language"; even citing to "Genesis." 2) The Court is also referring to "scientific knowledge" or "sciences" as creative forces of law to help ascertain whether there is a difference, and if there is a difference to what extent, between "impuissance," "impotence," and "wholly lacking in sexual power." As a conclusion, it can be said that the French and Louisiana lawmakers made no difference. 3) Therefore, reasoning a pari ratione, where disavowal is denied in case of "impotence," it is also denied should it be established that one is "wholly lacking in sexual power," such as suffering from "sterility." 4) Actually, relying on 18th and 19th centuries lawmakers to serve as a guide in reaching its decision in the 1970s, the Supreme Court will borrow the "understanding and reason" of these centuries to state: "We must nevertheless conclude that the greater includes the lesser—a fortiori ratione a minori ad majus." For the ancients "impotence" was the greater disability.*

   One could identify an attempt at reasoning "ab absurdum et ab inutilitate legis" in the sentence: "Why, then, should we believe they would have permitted disavowal when the husband actually fulfilled the conjugal union by coitus?" Since the lawmakers prohibited an action in disavowal when the husband could not perform the sex act, how could they possibly allow an action in disavowal when the father could perform the sexual act? It would be absurd to think in these terms.

F.   It is true that the husband's allegation is that he "is unable physically and biologically to produce spermatozoa." If we treat this as a well-pleaded fact, it could be argued that he should be allowed an opportunity to prove that fact in court. Three reasons militate against him. First, the public policy is against the attack on the paternity of the infant. The attack itself should be discouraged unless the likelihood of success is great. Second, the allegation is that the father is sterile (but not impotent) because of childhood diseases. The quality of proof required to sustain this conclusion (in the absence of surgical findings to which no hint is made) does not assure the success of the attack. Expert medical opinion evidence generally lacks the quality of certainty required to prove such a vital fact as parenthood. Third, since the husband has not alleged with particularity the "impediment to the natural maturity of petitioner's reproductive system," caused by the childhood diseases, we will treat his allegations as conclusions of the pleader, and not as material facts upon which his cause of action is based.

Comment: *the Supreme Court lists "three reasons [which] militate against" allowing the husband to prove that "he is unable physically and biologically to produce spermatozoa." It is worth referring back, at this point, to what we pointed out in our first comment and it is that the Supreme Court relied on its own jurisprudence first before referring to statutory law or Civil Code Articles in this instance. It is therefore logical for the Supreme Court to provide the fundamental reasons why its jurisprudence will remain, in this case, as it has been until now. The most important and decisive reason, in our opinion, is that of "the public policy against the attack on the paternity of the infant," or, as the Court will state further down in its opinion, "the benign policy of the State toward innocent children." It is an easy assumption to make that such were most likely the reasons [**ratio legis**] behind Civil Code Article 185 and that, therefore, such **ratio legis** pre-existed the Supreme Court's own jurisprudence. So, why not rely on the Civil Code as the primary source of law before referring to "jurisprudence," which is only a secondary source of law?*

G.   The same reasons for prohibiting disavowal of paternity for impotence seem to exist for prohibiting disavowal of paternity for sterility. If the scientific information available to lawyers and judges were clear and precise, to the effect that men are either sterile or fertile, with no degrees and shades of differences, it would be easy and perhaps sensible to conclude that our public policy should be different because we know so much more than the jurists of the early 19th century. If the state of the scientific knowledge were such that we could say without a doubt that this man is incapable of producing spermatozoa, then it might be justifiable for this court to make a change in the long-standing public policy of the State of Louisiana.

Comment: *1) The Court uses the method of reasoning called **a pari ratione** where it states, "the same reasons for prohibiting disavowal of paternity for impotence seem to exist for prohibiting disavowal of paternity for sterility." 2) In the next two sentences the Court will rely on the public policy or, we could say the* **Ratio Juris (Reason for the Jus or Law)** *of the whole law of marriage, paternity, filiation … to conclude that the progress of sciences, particularly medical sciences,* *has not been such as to be able to threaten or unsettle the "long standing public policy of the State of Louisiana." Another "legal" name for this long standing policy is **Ratio Juris** or "Reason for the Jus-Law in general" which is incorporated at the lower level of Civil Code Article 185 under the form of the **ratio legis** of that Article.*

It is somewhat surprising, to a civilian, to read here that the Supreme Court believes that "it might be justifiable for this Court to make a change in the long standing public policy of the State of Louisiana." Indeed, is it not the role and constitutional responsibility of the legislature rather than "this Court" to make any change in the public policy of the State?

H.   It may be that disavowal for 'accidental impotence' as contrasted to 'natural impotence' mentioned in C.C. 185 is not prohibited. As indicated by Planiol, supra, commentators were of the opinion that disavowal was not prohibited when the husband had suffered accidental or surgical emasculation, probably because of the quality of the evidence by which such 'impotence' could be proved. Before us, however, is a husband who only contends that a childhood disease prevented his production of spermatozoa. In view of the prohibition against disavowal on account of impotence, we believe his attack on the paternity of the infant is prohibited by C.C.185.

When we weigh the benign policy of the State toward innocent children against the mischief, scandal and difficulty of ascertaining the ultimate determinative facts, we conclude that it would be more appropriately a legislative function to change the policy of the State, if it is to be changed, at this time.

Comment: *1) In the first sentence, the Court could be said to have reasoned a* ***contrario sensu***, *pitting "accidental impotence v. natural impotence," where the Court referred to C.C. Article 185: since C.C.Art.185 mentioned expressly "natural impotence," reasoning* **a contrario sensu** *or* **inclusio unius, exclusio alterius***, it is obvious that "accidental impotence" was not meant to be mentioned. 2) The Court adds a reasoning* **ab auctoritate***, citing Planiol and other French commentators who were of the opinion that "accidental emasculation" or "surgical emasculation" were of such a nature that they were evidence of such a quality that "impotence could be proved." But such was not the case here since the father-husband did not undergo any accidental or surgical emasculation. 3) Moreover, "before us is a husband who only contends that a childhood disease prevented his production of spermatozoa." As regards this last statement, one could identify the Court's reasoning as going from the greater to the lesser or* **a fortiori ratione a majori ad minus***, where the word "only" suggests that a "disease" is even less likely to amount to emasculation than an accidental emasculation other than a surgical emasculation. 4) The Court is ultimately referring to La. C.C. Art. 185 as the source of law in* *the case. In this respect, the Court refers to "the benign policy of the State toward innocent children against the mischief, scandal and difficulty of ascertaining the ultimate determinative facts," as the "**ratio legis**" or reason for the law laid down in Art. 185. This same "**ratio legis**" is the foundation of the law governing the family created by marriage.*

I.   We hold that the prohibition of C.C. 185 against disavowal for 'natural impotence' also prohibits disavowal for sterility due to childhood disease.

Comment: *in this short holding, the Court mixes 1) a reasoning **in pari materia**, where it states that "natural impotence [and] and sterility due to childhood disease" are similar matters or physical conditions, 2) with an **a pari ratione** reasoning where it suggests that the **ratio legis** behind C.C.185 and "natural impotence" should be the same as an instance of sterility due to childhood disease. Thus, **ubi eadem ratio idem jus**, where the reason for denying a disavowal of paternity in the case of impotence is the same in the case of sterility, then the law of C.C.185 should be the law in that latter case also.*

BARHAM, Justice (dissenting)

J.   I do agree with the majority that sterility was very probably understood by the French in the Nineteenth Century and the redactors of our Civil Codes to be included within the term "impotence" or "l'impuissance." A distinction is drawn between the two in Bouvier's Law Dictionary (Rawle ed. 1897) in defining "impotence," but in defining "sterility" the terms are analogized: "Barrenness; incapacity to produce a child. It is curable and incurable; when of the latter kind at the time of the marriage, and arising from impotency, it is a good cause for dissolving a marriage. 1 Fodere , Me d.Le g. s 254. See IMPOTENCY." Even the latest edition of Black's Law Dictionary (3rd ed. 1944) recognized that the two terms are interrelated in stating that impotency "has also been used synonymously with 'sterility.'"

Comment: *1) Reasoning on the basis of the "history" of both French law and Louisiana law in the 19th c., and reasoning **ab auctoritate** (Bouvier's Law Dictionary), Justice Barham joins the majority when he writes "the term impotence included sterility." What is important here is that in his dissenting opinion, Justice Barham starts his reasoning from the same starting point as the majority to the effect that "sterility was very probably understood by the French in the Nineteenth Century and the redactors of our Civil Codes." Relying on the authority, **ab auctoritate,** of dictionaries, Justice Barham points out that all the words of concern here are defined in dictionaries. But definitions in such dictionaries are kind of "still" or "frozen" in the years they were written down; they are without life and confine the reader to the words that are used. On the other hand, the life of the law, the expression of the law, is in the jurisprudence. As Justice Barham* *will say further down in his dissent: "Basing its determination not to fairly adjudicate the issue before it solely upon an historical excursion into the past, the Court has not complied with the spirit of the Code or the letter of the Code in discharging the judicial function." 2) So, Justice Barham will dwell on the "spirit" of the law, the **ratio legis** and **ratio juris**" of La. C.C. Article 185 at stake here, as well as Article 312 of the French C.C.*

K.   More important than an attempt to find a current dictionary definition of 'impotence' would be a review of the French law for a definition of the term. The French jurisprudence in defining the term 'l'impuissance' has in an ever-increasing majority resolved that impotence does indeed encompass sterility and all forms of sexual disabilities which prevent procreation. Gebler, Le Droit Francais de la Filiation et la Ve rite (Paris 1970), fn 49, p. 157. Mme Gebler says: Nevertheless the courts have refused to consider only the letter of the text. They gave to article 312 the following meaning: 'incapacity to have sexual relations resulting in procreation.' Mayrand, 'La preuve de non-paternité,' in *La revue du barreau de la province de Québec*, 1965, p. 177(195), says that the jurisprudence of France employs a double tour de force: to similize sterility to impotence and illness to accident. At Fn 65 the following decisions of courts are cited: Lille, November 19, 1946; Bordeaux, February 7, 1951; Marseilles, July 23, 1953; Nancy, February 13, 1957.

   <u>Comment</u>: *in referring to the French jurisprudence as authority, **ab auctoritate**, Justice Barham makes the point that jurisprudence is a source of law as illustrated by the fact that "the French ... courts have refused to consider only the letter of the text" but, rather, have considered the spirit, or **ratio legis**, of the text to give the following meaning "to Article 312: incapacity to have sexual relations resulting in procreation." And there lies the spirit, the ratio, of the text of Article 312 of the French C.C. and Article 185 of the La. C.C.: **procreation**. Therefore, a man who cannot procreate, regardless of the cause, should have the right to disavow a child as not being his own.*

L.   Once we accept the conclusion that sterility is included within the term impotence, this case present an issue, which is res nova for this court. The first question to be considered is whether our law recognizes an action en desaveu on the ground of impotency, which is not 'natural.'

   <u>Comment</u>: *there are very interesting and crucial statements made here. First, Justice Barham seems to concede the point that "sterility is included in the term impotence." However, he immediately follows with the surprising and unexpected statement that "this case presents an issue which is res nova for this court." This was the proper and constructive statement to make because the emphasis will no longer be placed on "impotence" and, thus, "sterility," but on the adjective "nat-*

ural" which defines the kind of impotence that is included in "sterility." Hence the need to answer the question: "whether our law recognizes an action en désaveu on the ground of impotency which is "not natural""(our emphasis). In a certain way, from then on Justice Barham will use an a contrario reasoning on the adjective "natural" to dismiss its long accepted legal consequences when the impotence is "not natural." In the following paragraphs, Justice Barham will, quite logically, consider those instances where the impotence is "not natural," such as in the case of "accident," "surgery," or "illness." Hence his question: "What can constitute not natural impotence?"

M.   The language variations of Article 185 and its predecessors clearly indicate that under that article's present construction it was meant to allow the husband to proceed in an action for disavowal based upon impotence, sterility, infertility, or other medical basis which makes procreation impossible for him and which is an unnaturally acquired condition. The Civil Code of 1808 (Art. 7, par. 2) forbade an action en desaveu on the allegation of Accidental and natural impotency. This provision was apparently adopted with the idea of following the French in regard to natural impotency but of departing from the French recognition of allowing disavowal when the impotency of the husband was the effect of some accident (C.N. Art. 312). The Civil Code of 1825, however, included an amendment to that article without comment for the change. The prohibition of disavowal actions based upon accidental impotency was deleted (Art. 204). Since the adjective 'natural' was retained before the word 'impotence' and 'accidental' omitted in the 1825 Code and in our present Code of 1870, the obvious intent of this amendment was to exclude the prohibition against disavowal where accidental or unnatural cause produced 'impotence.'

<u>Comment</u>: *by highlighting the differences in the wording of the La. C.C. articles and the same articles in the French C.C., the dissenting opinion points to the "ratio," the reason or purpose behind these differences. Where the La. C.C. articles retained "natural" before the word "impotence" and omitted "accidental," the* **ratio***-reason was obviously to "exclude the prohibition against disavowal where accidental or unnatural cause produced impotence." This being the state of the law, Justice Barham will now challenge the majority in attempting to determine what can constitute unnatural impotence. The key words are now "natural" v. "unnatural" impotence. Justice Barham will reason from now on against the background of an* **a contrario sensu** *method of reasoning.*

N.   Believing that the right exists to bring an action en desaveu based upon sterility as well as inability to perform the sexual act when this inability is not of a natural origin, I find it necessary next to determine what can constitute unnatural impotence. The majority has said that Planiol states that 'accidental impotence' was not clearly defined in Article 312 of the French Civil Code. However, Planiol's discussion bears further consideration. It reads:

'The husband's impotence is recognized as a ground for disavowal only when it is the effect of some accident (Art. 312). What should be understood by 'accident'? Everybody agrees that the word applies to wounds and mutilations due to a fall, a combat, a surgical operation, or to any event of this nature. But should illness that may entail a prolonged prostration or weakness be classed among accidents? The question is an open one. The predominant view is that those who drafted the law had in mind a physical lesion due to an external cause. This excluded illness for its cause is internal. *But the words, 'by the effect of some accident,' have a most vague meaning. And it was formally said by Duveyrier, an orator of the Tribunat,*[192] *that a serious and prolonged illness could bring about physical impossibility as well as could wounds or mutilations. Locre Legislation civile, Vol. IV, p. 290). Toullier, Proudhon, Demante, Valette and Demolombe declared in that sense.'* (Emphasis supplied.) 1 Pt. 1 Planiol, Traite Elementaire de Droit Civil (trans. La.St.L.Inst. 1959) s 1433.

It appears that Planiol recognized that the majority of the doctrinal writers believed that illness and disease produce in certain cases impotence 'by the effect of some accident.' Baudry-Lacantinerie, who was of the view that the phrase 'de quelque accident' did not include impotence resulting from illness or disease, did admit that the majority of the doctrinaires held a belief to the contrary. 4 Baudry-Lacantinerie, Traite de Droit Civil (3E ed. 1907), s 482, p. 407. See also 5 Locre, Esprit du Code Napoléon pp. 28–36.

The current French jurisprudence and doctrine both support the view that impotence or sterility caused by illness and disease may be grounds for the action en desaveu. Gebler, op. cit. supra, p. 155, fn 38, quotes Merger, 'Etude juridique de l'insémination artificielle,' Bulletin de la Federation des societes de gynecologie, 1957, p. 319(323), for the proposition: No doubt that the strictness of the Code, prudent and wise in 1804, is unacceptable today; to permit a man to invoke an accident and to refuse him the right to invoke an illness is a piece of nonsense. All the courts, says Mme Gebler, which have passed upon this question have considered that an illness can entail the accidental impotence of Article 312.

---

192. The Tribunat was one of the Assemblies before which the French Civil Code was presented for their comments, observations, possible amendments ... before the Code could be adopted.

Comment: *referring back to the La. C.C. of 1808 (Art.7, par.2), to the French C.C. (C.N. Art.312) and to the authority of Planiol, Justice Barham will ask the question "what should be understood by accident?" This asks whether an accident can be the cause of "unnatural impotence. The next question will be, of course, whether "accident" and "illness" can be gathered together under the concept of "unnatural impotence." A reasoning in consimili casu or in pari materia can then be made and, thereby, lead to an a pari ratione reasoning. In support of his analysis, Justice Barham will use a reasoning ab auctoritate: "Locré," citing Duveyrier, "an orator at the Tribunat," Planiol, Baudry-Lacantinerie and Mrs Gebler, who wrote "all the courts which have passed upon this question have considered that an illness can entail the accidental impotence of Article 312."*

O.   Finding ourselves with a question that is res nova in our jurisdiction though there is ample jurisprudence interpreting the source of our paternity law, we should give weighty consideration to that jurisprudence and to the doctrine, which has evolved from it.

Comment: *this one sentence paragraph is a skilled transition, which states very clearly what role a court is called to play in a civilian jurisdiction. By stating that the issue before the Court is "res nova in our jurisdiction," Justice Barham means to embark upon an interpretation of the words of a code article that dates back to 1825 (then article 204 and thereafter article 185 of the Code of 1870), so as to give to these words a 20th century meaning. This can be done without violating the spirit or reason which presided over the drafting of the Civil Code of 1825 and its Article 204 (and Article 185 in the Code of 1870) when these articles retained the words "natural impotence" after having deleted the word "accidental impotence" of the Code of 1825. Hence the next paragraph:*

P.   Since we must only determine what is unnatural impotence as opposed to the possible French requirement of determining what is accidental impotence, we are not required to particularize the condition to fit the definition of 'accidental.' I submit that unnatural impotence is that impotence which is readily manifest when it occurs, which can be ascertained because of pathological, biological, or organic changes. It is therefore immaterial whether this change is made by mutilation through accident, by vasectomy through surgery, or by other means through illness or disease. The impotence need only be physically, medically, scientifically discernible with certainty. It is the certainty of the inability to procreate and not the nature of the disability that prevents procreation, which our Code intends as a criterion for disavowal for impotence.

Just as the French conclude that accidental impotence should not be limited to only external manifestation, I conclude that neither should impotence pro-

duced by illness and disease be denied as a ground because there is no external manifestation.

Comment: *1) At the outset, the dissenting opinion dismisses the need to articulate any meaning for the word "accident" since it is mentioned neither in
Art.204 of the La. C. C. of 1825 nor in Art. 185 of the La. C. C. of 1870 (in the
year 1972 of the case). The focus of the Justice's reasoning is on the meaning of
"unnatural impotence" by reasoning **a contrario sensu** on "natural impotence"
and reasoning literally or **ad verbum**, on "natural." These two methods of reasoning lead to the statement that* "unnatural impotence is that impotence which
is readily manifest when it occurs and which can be ascertained because of
pathological, biological or organic changes." *2) A reasoning **in pari materia**
follows where the Justice states that it is* "immaterial whether this change is made
by mutilation through accident, by vasectomy through surgery, or by other means
through illness or disease." *3) Lastly, it was important to have the support of a
reasoning **a pari ratione** to make the jump from "unnatural impotence" to include* "impotence because of illness or disease." *The reason why* "unnatural impotence" *can be a ground for disavowal of paternity is because of* "the certainty
of the inability to procreate" *and that certainty is* "a criterion for disavowal for
impotence." *That reason, i.e., that certainty of the inability to procreate, exists
just as well in the case of impotence or sterility caused by illness or disease. This
a pari ratione reasoning appears clearly in the statement*: "Just as the French conclude that accidental impotence should not be limited to only external manifestation, I conclude that neither should impotence produced by illness and disease
be denied as a ground because there is no external manifestation."

Q.   It is an incongruity that the majority recognizes the magnificent strides
made in medical science in this area by comparing present achievements with
Nineteenth Century knowledge, and yet refuses to allow this man the opportunity to resort to new sources of knowledge.

Comment: *can we go as far as saying that the majority was "illogical," not to
say that it made an **ab absurdum** reasoning where it recognized "the manifest
strides in medical science" and "yet refuses to allow this man the opportunity to
resort to new sources of knowledge"?*

R.   The use of exegetical approach in isolation does not discharge the judicial obligation when our court works to and through the Code. While exegesis is certainly helpful, often very enlightening, it can entomb the court
and the law in the darkness of the past. The combination of the exegetical,
the empirical, and the functional methods of interpretation is required in
order that the law serve the people, that the law be a reflection of the people's
understanding, desires, and needs ... In Techniques of Judicial Interpretation

in Louisiana, 22 La.L.Rev. 727, Mr. Justice Tate said that where the formal wording itself has not provided a rule of law, the objective and functional methods of interpretation which look to policy considerations and the general purpose of the legislation are most effective ... The exegetical approach 'paralyzed the judge' and prevents him from determining the legal rights of man in a world unknown to the lawmakers who framed the Code. Following the lead of Gény, the French judiciary moved to the 'free scientific research' approach ... We are a civilian jurisdiction, and we should as a court follow that tradition.

Comment: *there are some shortcomings of a purely "exegetical approach" to codal interpretation. It paralyses judges and prevents them "from determining the legal rights of man in a world unknown to the lawmakers who framed the Code." Because we are in a civilian jurisdiction, the judiciary should follow the lead of Gény and move to the free scientific approach.*

S.		What change in policy is needed here to reach the result this dissent offers? What has been the policy of the state on disavowal for sterility? The courts have been silent. The Code is silent. A functional approach supports the policy I advocate. Comparative law analysis supports that policy. The issue before us must be decided, and it cannot be deferred to legislative counsel. Basing its determination not to fairly adjudicate the issue before it solely upon an historical excursion into the past, the court has not complied with the spirit of the Code or the letter of the Code in discharging the judicial function.

As our Code says, the most important consideration is to determine the true meaning, reason, and spirit of a law. Surely the vast majority of the people—and this would be reflected in their legislative representatives—would find it almost unfathomable that the law would allow disavowal for impotence but not for sterility. Is this fine distinction valid? Does it serve any purpose? Is it the custom of the people as reflected in their mental processes? Is this distinction the public policy of this state? Does the public believe and understand that one condition justifies bastardy and the other does not?

The majority recognized that the legal issue between the parties to this litigation was whether this husband should be able to attempt to establish that he was naturally sterile so that he could not have been the father of the child of his wife. The majority makes a legislative policy determination that the 'prohibition' against disavowal for "natural impotence" also prohibits disavowal for sterility due to childhood disease.' That prohibition is not contained in the Code. I believe it to be a holding contrary to the public's belief and understanding and contrary to public policy as expressed in the Code.

__Comment__: *a few paragraphs above, Justice Barham stated that the issue be-fore the Court was "__res nova.__" He comes back here to that statement but in a sweep-ing way where he writes, "[t]he courts have been silent. The Code is silent."*[193] *Then he criticizes the majority for not having acted as it should have acted in fill-ing the blank, the silence in the Code. His criticism is somewhat harsh when he writes, the "court has not complied with the spirit of the Code or the letter of the Code in discharging the judicial function." The two important words here are: "__spirit__" and "__letter.__" Indeed, all methods of reasoning are based either on the let-ter of the law or the spirit/reason of the law. For Justice Barham the majority failed in both respects because it made "a legislative policy determination that the pro-hibition against disavowal for natural impotence also prohibits disavowal for steril-ity due to childhood disease." Justice Barham is clearly saying, in the first place, that the majority has usurped the legislative function by formulating what the Jus-tice called "a legislative policy prohibiting disavowal for sterility due to childhood disease" when such a "prohibition is not contained in the Code"; in the second place, Justice Barham is making it very clear that there is a public policy expressed in the Code, that that policy should obviously prevail, particularly when the pub-lic policy of the Code is "contrary" to that expressed by the majority.*

Dorothy Hebert Ardoin et al.

v.

Hartford Accident and Indemnity Co. et al.

Supreme Court of Louisiana[194]

Facts [from the Opinion]:

In this case, we are called upon to decide if Louisiana courts are governed by the "locality rule" in determining whether an act of a medical specialist that causes damage to his patient constitutes fault, which obliges the physician to re-pair it.

On July 9, 1976, Lorrie Ardoin died during a "coronary artery by-pass" oper-ation, which was being performed by Dr. James Bozeman, a cardiovascular surgeon, at Our Lady of Lourdes Hospital in Lafayette, Louisiana. This type of operation requires that the patient's heart be stopped and that his vital func-tions be maintained by a "heart-lung" machine throughout the surgery. The

---

193. We would have much preferred for Justice Barham to have reversed the order of his references here. The Code, as the primary source of law, should have come first. Fur-thermore, had there been no Code article, this case would not have existed.

194. 360 So. 2d 1331 (1978).

apparatus consists of a pump with tubes, which are used to suction blood from the patient's body and return it to his arteries after the blood has been oxygenated. This process is known as cardiopulmonary perfusion and the hospital attendants who operate the heart-lung machine are called perfusionists. Coincidentally with Ardoin's operation, the hospital initiated the use of new tubing manufactured by Bentley Laboratories, Inc. in its cardiopulmonary perfusion. Because the hospital previously used another medical supplier's tubing, Bentley Laboratories' district manager, Travis Bohannon, was present during the operation for the purpose of assisting Darrell Gregory and Ronald DeBlanc, the hospital perfusionists, in attaching the new tubing to the heart-lung machine. After the cardiopulmonary apparatus had been assembled and the surgery was underway, Dr. Bozeman attached one of the tubes to the ventricle of the patient's heart for the purpose of pumping blood from the patient into the oxygenator. Instead of suctioning blood, as it should have, however, the tube pumped air into Ardoin's heart. Death followed instantaneously when a massive air embolism reached the patient's brain.

The decedent's wife and nine children brought a wrongful death action alleging various acts of negligence on the part of the following defendants: Dr. James Bozeman, the cardiovascular surgeon; Darrell E. Gregory, perfusionist; Ronald DeBlanc, perfusionist; Our Lady of Lourdes Hospital; Travis Bohannon, district manager for Bentley Laboratories, Inc.; and Bentley Laboratories, Inc. Numerous third party demands were filed by the defendants and their insurers. Our review is limited to the third party action filed by Travis Bohannon, Bentley Laboratories, Inc. and its insurers against Dr. Bozeman.

In an effort to prove negligence on the part of Dr. Bozeman in not testing the tube before inserting it into Ardoin's heart, the third party plaintiffs sought to introduce the testimony of Dr. Prentiss Smith, a cardiovascular surgeon. Because Dr. Smith practiced in Baton Rouge and was not familiar with the care or skill of cardiovascular surgeons in Lafayette, the trial judge ruled that Dr. Smith was not a competent witness.

Upon conclusion of the trial, the jury found negligence on the part of Gregory, one of the perfusionists, and Bohannon, the district manager of Bentley Laboratories. No negligence was found by the jury on the part of Dr. Bozeman.

We granted writs on behalf of third party plaintiff Bohannon, his employer and their insurers, to review the questions of law raised by the exclusion of Dr. Smith's testimony, viz., whether the interpretation of the law as to a physician's duty to his patient was correctly set forth in Meyer v. St. Paul-Mercury Indemnity Co.; whether the law in this regard was altered by La.R.S. 9:2794; and, if so, whether the legislation applies to quasi-offenses occurring before its effective date.

Opinion

DENNIS, Justice

A.   The standard of conduct required of persons in Louisiana in their relationships with one another is stated in simple, general terms set forth in Article 2315 of the Louisiana Civil Code of 1870: "Every act whatever of man that causes damage to another obliges him by whose fault it happened to repair it …"

This single article forms the basis of all tort liability in Louisiana. The remaining articles of the Civil Code's chapter of legal principles regulating offenses and quasi-offenses, Articles 2316 through 2324, contain amplifications as to what constitutes "fault" and under what circumstances a defendant may be held liable for his act or that of a person or thing for which he is responsible.

Under the civilian tradition of our state, the courts have been given a broad, general principle of legislative will from which they are required to determine when the interest of society is best served by requiring one who harms another to respond in damages for the injury caused. In deciding whether the conduct in a specific case falls below that in which a person can engage without becoming responsible for resultant damage, a court must refer first to the fountainhead of responsibility, Article 2315, and next in applying the article to the many other articles in our code which deal with the responsibility of certain persons or that which arises due to certain types of activity. After searching through the code itself a jurist should refer in turn to the acts of the legislature, local governments, and other legislative and administrative bodies. Then, having explored the legislative and administrative sources of standards of proper conduct, a court should turn next to the experience of the judiciary in the interpretation and application of these standards to actual situations.

Comment: *we have opted to select this long excerpt for the reason that Justice Dennis, from the very beginning of his opinion, places the emphasis on "the civilian tradition of our state" as regards the hierarchy of the sources of law in the State of Louisiana. First in the ranking or hierarchy of the sources of law in "the civilian tradition of our state" comes* **statutory law or code articles** *(2315 through 2324). Then, in combination with these articles, the purpose, reason and "the principles" must be brought to the forefront so as to be used to interpret these* *code articles. It follows as a logical and fundamental consequence of that distri-bution of powers in a civil law jurisdiction that* "the courts [of our state] have been given a broad, general principle of legislative will from which they are required to determine when the interest of society is best served by requiring one who harms another to respond in damages for the injury caused." *[We want to point out here that Justice Dennis is referring to the legislative will as the constitutional power responsible for laying down general principles for the interest of society or the public policies that will best serve society. The courts must, therefore, find in these principles or public policies their reasons for decid-ing cases].* In addition to or in lieu of the Civil Code, "after searching through the code itself, a <u>jurist</u> (our emphasis) should refer in turn to the acts of the legislature, local governments, and other legislative and administrative bod-ies." *In other words, the jurist must turn, after the Civil Code, to other "primary sources of law."* It is only "[t]hen, having explored the legislative and admin-istrative sources of standard of proper conduct, a court should turn next to the experience of the judiciary in the interpretation and application of these standards to actual situations." *As Justice Dennis makes it clear,* "the experience of the judiciary" *is a secondary source of law.*

B.   In deciding the issue before us the lower courts did not follow the process of referring first to the code and other legislative sources but treated lan-guage from a judicial opinion as the primary source of law. This is an indication that the position of the decided case as an illustration of past experience and the theory of the individualization of decision have not been properly understood by our jurists in many instances. Therefore, it is important that we plainly state that, particularly in the changing field of delictual responsibility, the notion of Stare decisis, derived as it is from the common law, should not be thought con-trolling in this state. The case law is invaluable as previous interpretation of the broad standard of Article 2315, but it is nevertheless secondary information.

Comment: *in this excerpt, the Supreme Court will dwell on the "civilian tra-dition" of ranking the sources of law that was intentionally referred to in the prior excerpt. In doing so, the Supreme Court, in a certain manner, reprimands "the lower courts" for having followed too closely "the common law notion of stare de-cisis." And the Supreme Court adds that "case law is invaluable.... but it is nev-ertheless secondary information."*

C.   Starting first with the keystone for tort responsibility in Louisiana, Ar-ticle 2315, we notice that it places no geographical or occupational limitations on the notion of "fault." Likewise, Article 2316 speaks very broadly of every person's responsibility for the damage he shall occasion "not merely by his act, but by his negligence, his imprudence, or his want of skill." Under these articles, a medical specialist who injures a patient through his negligence, imprudence or want of skill must respond in damages. The code does not in any of its articles condition recovery by an injured patient upon proof of the physician's fault in relation to the medical standard of care or skill within a particular community or locality. Accordingly, the code itself does not provide for special or localized definitions of negligence, imprudence or want of skill by doctors.

Comment: *having laid out the hierarchy of the sources of law to be used in this case, the Supreme Court now begins its interpretation of these sources.*

1) The Supreme Court begins with a broad, expansive reading of La. C.C. Articles 2315 and 2316. The method of reasoning used by the Court on these articles is based on the words, the grammar and the syntax of the articles. Thus reasoning **a generali sensu** *or* **ubi lex non distinguit nec nos distinguere debemus** *on Articles 2315 and 2316 the Supreme Court is led to say that the article(s) places "no geographical or occupational limitations on the notion of fault. Likewise, Article 2316 speaks very broadly of every person's responsibility for the damage he shall occasion not merely by his act, but by his negligence, his imprudence, or his want of skill." Thus, where the law makes no distinction, we should make no distinction either. It is easy then for the Court to conclude by saying that "under these articles, a medical specialist who injures a patient through his negligence, imprudence or want of skill must respond in damages."*

2) In this same paragraph, the Court makes a practical application of reasoning **a generali sensu** *when it uses the word "man" in Article 2315 cited above and the word "person" in Article 2316 to mean that either word applies to the general practitioner as well as to the specialist; they are "persons" to begin with and the law of these Code articles looks at men "en masse," as a whole and not as "individuals." The law of the Civil Code is not a "personal law."*

3) Lastly, inspired by the same frame of mind that leads it to look at the words "in general" and broadly, the Supreme Court abolishes the frontiers between the "general practitioner" and the "specialist," frontiers which are nowhere mentioned in the Civil Code articles. The Civil Code is concerned neither with "geography" nor with "specialization." The Code contemplates only the liability of a "man" or of a "person." There is no adjective of any kind that precedes any of these words in the Civil Code. An interpreter of the Civil Code, such as a judge, should not, therefore, add an adjective where none exists in a "primary source of law" like the Civil Code.

Turning to Act 807 of 1975 which became La. R. S. 9:2794, the Court states that:

D.   The legislature enacted legislation apparently intended to have an effect of this sort upon the proof of fault by physicians and dentists not engaged in a specialized practice. The statute expressly states that a patient who has been damaged by the act or omission of a physician or dentist must prove the degree of knowledge or skill possessed or the degree of care ordinarily exercised by physicians or dentists practicing in the same community or locality in which the defendant practices.

Comment: *the Supreme Court points to the "reason" behind Act 807 as applying to "physicians or dentists not engaged in a specialized practice ... practicing in the same community or locality in which the defendant practices." The Court is combining here a reasoning **stricto sensu**[195] (applying the clear and unambiguous words of the law, as per La. C.C. Art.9), with an **a generali sensu** reasoning on the basis of La. C. C. Art. 11 with a particular emphasis on "words of art and technical terms." In addition, the Court adds to the weight of its reasoning by identifying the "reason" behind Act 807 to make a restrictive use of it (reasoning **ratione legis stricta**) so that only non-specialist practitioners are governed by the Act.*

E.   In contrast with the standard of conduct and burden of proof affecting practitioners not engaged in a specialty, the statute further provides that where the defendant practices in a particular specialty and where the alleged acts of medical negligence raise issues peculiar to the particular medical specialty involved, then the plaintiff "has the burden of proving the degree of care ordinarily practiced by physicians or dentists within the involved medical specialty." Thus, the legislature has provided guidance in applying the Civil Code's general principle of fault to the acts of a particular medical specialist by directing that they be measured by the degree of care ordinarily practiced by others involved in the same specialty. Unlike the statute's standard of care for practitioners not engaged in a specialty, the specialist's duty is not governed by the professional standard within a particular locality or community.

Comment: *turning to the case of practitioners in a particular specialty, the Court makes, again, a literal reading of the statute as required by La. C. C. Articles 9 and 11.One can also say that the Court is making an **a contrario** reasoning where it states that "unlike the statute's standard of care for practitioners not engaged in a specialty, the specialist's duty is not governed by the professional standard within a*

---

195. See *Dictionary of the Civil Code*, LexisNexis, 2014; word: **Stricto sensu**: Lat. Expression meaning "in the strict sense" (of a word); is commonly used in the interpretation of legislation or agreements to follow closely the narrow sense of the text and confine its application within these limit. Ex. delict, *stricto sensu*/in its strict sense, refers to an intentional delict, as opp. to a quasi-delict.

particular locality or community." In other words, what was written about the "same community or locality" about a general practitioner, was not written about the specialist. Thus, the community or locality rule does not apply to the specialist.

F.   The court of appeal read the statute differently and concluded that it impliedly provides localized definitions of negligence, imprudence and want of skill by medical specialists. This erroneous interpretation resulted from a misapprehension of the civilian nature of our delictual responsibility laws as well as a disregard of the rules for their interpretation set forth in Articles 13–20 of the Civil Code.

Instead of beginning with the keystone of responsibility, Article 2315, and reading La. R.S. 9:2794 in the light of it and other pertinent articles, the intermediate court approached the problem as one of deciding the extent, if any, to which the jurisprudence had been amended by the legislative act. Thus, rather than reading La. R.S. 9:2794 as the lawmakers' indication of how the basic principle of Article 2315, as amplified by Article 2316, should be applied in a particular class of cases, the appeals court measured the enactment solely against language contained in a judicial opinion. The basic error in this method of interpretation is that it not only ignores the first principles of our law but it also assumes that jurisprudence is equivalent to legislation instead of treating it as judicial interpretation which may or may not adequately reflect the meaning of the laws for contemporary purposes.

Comment: *the Supreme Court is reminding the lower courts of the ranking of the sources of law in the civilian tradition when the Court states that "this erroneous interpretation resulted from a misapprehension of the civilian nature of our delictual responsibility laws as well (now Articles 9–13)." Therefore the statute cannot be read as the Court of Appeal applied the statute to medical specialists. The Supreme Court is even more critical of the Court of Appeal where it blames "the intermediate court for having approached the problem as one of deciding the extent, if any, to which the jurisprudence had been amended by the legislative act." How can a Louisiana court suggest that a statute amended a court decision or the jurisprudence? In a civil law jurisdiction a statute can amend another statute, i.e., a rule of law of the same nature and equal rank but it cannot amend a court decision, which is of a lower rank and of a different and lesser binding legal force. "The basic error in this method of interpretation is that it not only ignores the first principles of our law but it also assumes that jurisprudence is equivalent to legislation instead of treating it as judicial interpretation which may or may not adequately reflect the meaning of the laws for contemporary purposes."*

G.   On the other hand, adherence to civilian theory requires a jurist to begin with the broad principle of Article 2315 that everyone must repair the damage caused by his fault, and with the amplification of Article 2316 that fault includes everyone's negligence, imprudence or want of skill as measured against a general standard of conduct. Due notice next should be taken of our constitution's virtual prohibition of local legislation and the lack of any geographical differentiation between physicians licensed in Louisiana under the medical practice act.

Comment: *after having stated, once again, what is the civilian approach to the sources of law in a codified system of law, the Supreme Court stresses now that the process of codification is a means or a technique of drafting that enables the codifier to write the law in the form of principles or general standards of conduct. This is particularly true here where Article 2315 states "that* everyone *must repair the damage caused by his* fault*" (emphasis ours). Thus, this broad principle must be read* **a generali sensu**. *In addition, it is tied to another principle which addresses the concept of fault as including "everyone's negligence, imprudence or want of skill as measured against a general standard of conduct." By placing such an emphasis on these principles, one dealing with "everyone" and the other with "fault," the Court gives a very strong hint that the "reason" behind these principles will strengthen and justify their broad application. In a sense, at this point in time in this decision, a "specialist" would have understood that the odds were going to be against him!*

Calling upon the "constitution's virtual prohibition of local legislation and the lack of any geographical differentiation between physicians licensed in Louisiana under the medical practice act," *the Supreme Court makes use, once again, of a reasoning* **a generali sensu** *to say rather specifically, that where the law makes no distinction we are not to make any, or* **ubi lex non distinguit, nec nos distinguere debemus.**

H.   A comparison should be made of the laws prescribing uniform standards of competence or conduct for other professions or classes of occupations.

Comment: *here is a good illustration of reasoning both* **in pari materia** *(where the court will refer, in a footnote, to attorneys, nurses, pharmacists …) and* **a pari ratione** *or* **a simili ratione**. *The reason behind the statutes applicable to attorneys, nurses and others is the same as the reason for a rule of law applicable to medical practitioners. No distinction is to be made on account of geography, locality as the interest of society, the public interest, require.*

I.   At this point, a tenet of our legal philosophy becomes apparent, i.e., that civil and criminal sanctions imposed for socially unacceptable conduct should be applied equally throughout the state to all citizens within the same class or set of circumstances. Therefore, one must conclude that, if the legislature were to act contrary to this policy by establishing a different definition of negligence, imprudence or want of skill by a medical specialist within each locality, the lawmaking body would express its intention explicitly. Since La. R.S. 9:2794 contains no such expression pertaining to medical specialists, the statute should not be given the effect of Balkanizing those representing themselves as having superior skill or knowledge beyond that common to the medical profession by the application of varying geographic standards of fault.

Comment: *these statements by the Supreme Court are the "core," or the "heart," of the whole opinion. The Court raises the level of its legal analysis from "legislation" or "**lex**" (written rules of law) to "**Law**" or "**Jus**" (unwritten source of law such as natural law, equity, reason). The "**ratio**," or reason, on which the Court relies is not a reason extracted from legislation, a written rule of law, or a "**ratio legis**" but a reason based on* "a tenet of our legal philosophy," *which* "becomes apparent, i.e., that civil and criminal sanctions imposed for socially unacceptable conduct should be applied equally throughout the state to all citizens within the same class or set of circumstances." *Such is the "**Ratio Juris**" of which the **ratio legis** of Act 807, or the **ratio legis** of La. C.C. Articles 2315–2316 are a legislative expression. On the basis of this principle or **Ratio Juris** as the fountainhead of liability and controlling here, the Supreme Court will, very logically and rationally, use a reasoning **ubi eadem ratio idem jus**, or where the reason is the same the law ought to be the same, to conclude* "that, if the legislature were to act contrary to this policy by establishing a different definition of negligence, imprudence or want of skill by a medical specialist within each locality, the lawmaking body would express its intention explicitly."

J.   Furthermore, an application of the Civil Code rules of statutory construction leads to the same conclusion. As the court of appeal opinion plainly reflects, words must be added by the court to the portion of the statute pertaining to medical specialists in order to tie the standard of conduct prescribed therein to the locality rule. Such an interpretation tends to disregard the expression of the legislative will. Courts must give to the words used by the legislature the meaning they are ordinarily understood to have, and when the law is clear and free from any ambiguity, the letter of it must not be disregarded under the pretext of pursuing its spirit. La. C.C. arts. 13, 14.

Since the meaning of the law is not dubious, it is unnecessary to consider the reason and spirit of it cf. La. C.C. art. 18, but a survey of the possible considerations underlying its enactment confirms our interpretation.

Comment: *a statement, once again, about the ranking of the sources of law and the application of the Code articles on the interpretation of a clear and unambiguous law. It is neither the role nor the duty of the courts to add words to a statute, in order to bring facts un-provided for or sets of facts different from those of the* *statute under the scope of application of the words of that statute. By adding words to the statute on general practitioners so as to include specialists, "such an interpretation tends to disregard the expression of the legislative will." The legislative will being the primary source of law, "the words used by the legislature [must be given] the meaning they are ordinarily understood to have." The courts cannot "pursue the spirit of the law" when the "law is clear and free from any ambiguity."*

K.   By refusing to adopt a standard tied to locality for specialists, the legislature simply may have chosen to recognize the realities of medical life. The various medical specialties have established uniform requirements for certification. The national boards dictate the length of residency training, subjects to be covered, and the examinations given to the candidates for certification. Thus, the medical profession itself recognizes national standards for specialists that are not determined by geography. Indeed, whatever may have justified a locality rule for physicians fifty or a hundred years ago cannot be reconciled with the actualities of medical practice today. The quality of medical school training has improved dramatically. With modern transportation and communication systems, new techniques and discoveries are available to all doctors within a short period of time through seminars, medical journals, closed circuit television presentations, special radio networks for doctors, tape-recorded digests of medical literature, and current correspondence courses.

Comment: *1) In this excerpt, the Court does make use of a reasoning **in pari materia** where the Court refers to "the various medical specialties," including the specialty of concern in this case, cardiovascular surgeons. All the different specialties have "national standards" thereby rejecting the application of the geographic/locality rule "today." 2) One can identify here a difficult method of reasoning to resort to and it is reasoning **ab absurdum** or **ab inutilitate legis**. Indeed, the Court refers to "the actualities of medical practice today ... [to] modern transportation and communication systems, new techniques and discoveries are available to all doctors.... seminars, medical journals, closed circuit television presentations ..." It would make no sense to apply today a rule of law enacted several years ago under very different circumstances. The locality rule does not make much sense today. 3) After the Court used these methods of reasoning, it was logical for the Court to call upon an **a pari ratione** or **ubi eadem ratio idem jus** reasoning to hold cardiovascular surgeons to the same national standard of care as "various medical specialties that have established uniform requirements for certification."*

L.   It is generally recognized that a rule of law, which restricts proof of medical negligence to a standard of care within a locality, tends to promote three evils: (1) It may effectively immunize from liability any doctor who happens to be the sole practitioner in his community. "He could be treating bone fractures by the application of wet grape leaves and yet remain beyond the criticism of more enlightened practitioners from other communities;" (2) The practitioners in a community are able to establish the standard of care which could, perhaps, be an inferior one; (3) A "conspiracy of silence" in the plaintiff's locality could effectively preclude any possibility of obtaining expert medical testimony. Because fewer specialists than generalists are likely to be found in most communities, the potential for these detrimental effects would only be exacerbated by extending the locality rule to specialists.

Comment: *the Court makes here a very good reasoning **ab absurdum** and **ab inutilitate legis**. By pointing out that by restricting* "proof of medical negligence to a standard of care within a locality [it is] to promote three evils: (1).... (2).... (3) ..." *It would be absurd to uphold the locality rule. A rule of law cannot be based on such an "absurd" outcome, as "the potential for these detrimental effects would only be exacerbated by extending the locality rule to specialists."*

M.   In recognition of the locality rule's possible harsh consequences and the fact that the practice of medicine by certified specialists within most medical specialties is similar throughout the country, many jurisdictions have abandoned entirely the locality rules as to specialists. Bruni v. Tatsumi, 46 Ohio St.2d 127, 346 N.E.2d 673 (1976); Shilkret v. Annapolis Emergency Hospital Association, 276 Md. 187, 349 A.2d 245 (1975); Shier v. Freedman, 58 Wis.2d 269, 206 N.W.2d 166 (1973); Naccarato v. Grob, 384 Mich. 248, 180 N.W.2d 788 (1970); Wiggins v. Piver, 276 N.C. 134, 171 S.E.2d 393 (1970); Kronke v. Danielson, 108 Ariz. 400, 499 P.2d 156 (1972); Brune v. Belinkoff, 354 Mass. 102, 235 N.E.2d 793 (1968). This is consistent with the position advocated by the American Law Institute. Restatement of Torts (Second) s 299A (1965) (comment d).

Moreover, only a distinct minority of states still adhere to the strict locality rule. Dunham v. Elder, 18 Md.App. 360, 306 A.2d 568 (1973); Gandara v. Wilson, 85 N.M. 161, 509 P.2d 1356 (1973); Levett v. Etkund, 158 Conn. 567, 265 A.2d 70 (1969); Lockart v. Maclean, 77 Nev. 210, 361 P.2d 670 (1961). A plurality of states now apply the "similar locality" rule, See, e. g., Mecham v. McLeay, 193 Neb. 457, 227 N.W.2d 829 (1975); Karrigan v. Nazareth Convent & Academy, Inc., 212 Kan. 44, 510 P.2d 190 (1973); Runyon v. Reid, 510 P.2d 943 (Okl.1973); Burton v. Smith, 34 Mich.App. 270, 191 N.W.2d 77 (1971); Incollingo v. Ewing, 444 Pa. 263, 299, 282 A.2d 206 (1977); whereas some courts have extended geographic boundaries to include those centers readily accessible for appropriate treatment. See, Gist v. French, 136 Cal.App.2d 247, 288 P.2d 1003 (1955); Josselyn v. Dearborn, 148 Me. 328, 62 A.2d 174 (1948);

Tvedt v. Haugen, 70 N.D. 338, 294 N.W. 183 (1940); cf. Pederson v. Du-mouchel, 72 Wash.2d 73, 431 P.2d 973 (1967).

Comment: *here is an example of extensive reasoning **ab auctoritate**. To support its holding of doing away with the application of the locality rule to specialists, the Court is obviously relying on the authority attached to "many jurisdictions" of other states, as well as the authority of the American Law Institute. On the other hand, "only a distinct minority of states still adhere to 'the strict locality rule'" or the "similar locality" rule.*

N.   Although as noted by the court of appeal, La. R.S. 9:2794 was enacted as part of a legislative campaign to provide the medical profession with additional protection from occupational litigation, there is no justification for assuming that every sentence in this body of laws must be construed against its obvious meaning and in favor of the interest group, which it generally benefits. Casual observation tells us that all legislation is founded on the principle of mutual concession. To interpret a statute in a totally one-sided manner simply because it was introduced and passed at the behest of one class of citizens may in effect read out of the law compromises, which were crucial to its enactment. There is no logical reason why the legislature could not have intended to afford various protections to the medical profession and at the same time reject the idea of localized standards of conduct as to specialists. It is evident, in fact, that a locality rule for specialists would not be rooted in reality.

Comment: *in its conclusion on the scope of application of the statute of concern here, the Court returns to the "reason" behind the statute. It calls upon common sense, logic and reality to conclude "that a locality rule for specialists would not be rooted in reality."*

Arrêts and Arrêtistes

[Neil Duxbury, An Essay on Influence, Oxford 2001]

"The emergence of case note writing as a general phenomenon in France can be traced back to the 1840s, during which decade there were inaugurated a number of journals devoted to the reporting and the analysis of judicial decisions.[…]

The journals which began to appear in the 1840s were usually the joint ventures of academic and practicing lawyers, and the case notes which they contained were the product of, and were intended to be of interest to both constituencies.[…] The fact that, in nineteenth century France, case notes were produced not only by academic but also by practicing lawyers—and even, occasionally by judges—provides, Meynial believes, part of the explanation as to why the worlds of the academic lawyer on the one hand and the practitioner and judge on the other have not, traditionally, been all that far apart. For the basic purpose if case note writing was not only to analyse case law—to try to uncover and explain the rationale behind decisions and to examine how, or if, particular outcomes might be reconciled with those reached in earlier or analogous cases—but also to consider whether existing legal commentary or *doctrine* might indicate how, in the future, judges might advance *la jurisprudence* still further. Thus it is that Meynial ascribed to the efforts of *les arrêtistes* a distinctly constructive, dialectical function: through commentary on cases, academics, practitioners and judges were able to promote the complementary development of *jurisprudence* and *doctrine*, of case law and legal writing. […] Dawson observes that in the French legal context, case notes:

'perform the same function as a forum for free criticism and exchange of views. Being comments on the cases reported, they address themselves to specific issues, to all the nuances in the facts, to the motives for the decision whether expressed or veiled, and to the possibilities of reconciling results with those in earlier cases, by distinctions or otherwise. The analytical note is also expected to assemble all the resources of doctrine, to criticize and evaluate it in its bearing on the specific problem. It is an extremely flexible instrument, expressing the skill, learning and insight of individual authors but requiring them to address themselves to the interests and needs of practitioners as well as to those of their academic colleagues'.

[...]

The most prolific and important of the nineteenth century case note writers was the law professor, J.E. Labbé. Between the appearance of his first case note in 1859, and his death in 1894, Labbé published, mainly in *Sirey*, literally hundreds of influential notes on cases covering more or less the entire spectrum of French private law. 'He and others like him', Dawson remarks, 'discovered for themselves and revealed to their colleagues the depth, richness, and complexity of the gloss the courts had laid on the codes'. This vibrant tradition of French case note writing carried over into the twentieth century.

[...]

Just as Labbé had led the way in the nineteenth century, twentieth century *arrêtistes* such as Josserand, Planiol, Capitant and Waline continued to use the case note as a medium through which to consider the implications and possible shortcomings of, as well as the reasons behind and doctrinal background to, the decisions of courts. The principal art of case note writing, Carbonnier observes, is to consider the exercise as an opportunity to try to influence judicial though in the future by highlighting, in view of what a court has already decided, alternative outcomes, approaches and lines of reasoning. Thus it is that, in France, the modern case note has provided feedback to the judiciary— a judiciary which is generally responsive to, and sometimes prepared to participate in, academic dialogue.

[...]

Indeed, as Deguergue remarks, the *arrêtiste* may sometimes serve as an '*auxiliaire du juge*'.

[...]

Why has the tradition of case note writing in France been so venerated and influential? In England the case note is commonly considered to be one of the lowliest forms of legal literature, not least because the case notes section of the law journal often provide a nursery slope for the tyro academic who has yet to find either the time or the confidence to engage in more sustained research. In the USA, the case commentaries, frequently article-length by English standards, which appear in certain of the law school journals are invariably written by student editors. Most American law professors would consider the writing of such commentaries to be rather beneath them. Why then, in France, has the case note been elevated so?

There are at least four possible answers to this question. First of all, case note writing is a valuable marketing strategy for those French academics who seek to supplement their salaries by acting as *consultants* on behalf of *avocats*. The writer of a case note will very often possess specialist knowledge, having written his or her thesis on the specific branch of law with which the note deals. [...] Secondly, French case note writers are rarely legal novices. Case note writing tends to be a task of privilege, a mark of distinction. Part of the reason for this—and this is our third answer—is that French case notes are highly visible.

[...]

The juxtapositioning of cases and case notes not only means that the latter are more likely to be read by legal practitioners and judges but also that the most incisive notes are unlikely to go unappreciated, for the notes appear as immediate responses to the outcome and so lend themselves to easy comparison with the actual judgements. Case notes thus provide legal commentators with the opportunity to operate as shadow-judges, to showcase their doctrinal skills and to try to influence judicial thinking in the future. It hardly seems surprising that the distinguished academic lawyer should normally revel in the role of *l'arrêtiste*.

The fourth answer to the question which we have posed relates to the professional status of the distinguished academic lawyer. Historically, as we have already noted, the law faculty and the judiciary in France have enjoyed a fairly close relationship. This relationship remains close to this day.

[...]

French legal culture is by no means indifferent to academic lawyers and their view-points.

That successful French legal academics are often respected and sought out for their expertise and judgments makes them somewhat similar to their North American counterparts. We have seen, however, that many American law professors produce scholarship which judges do not find particularly useful. Legal commentary in France, by contrast, tends to be less abstruse and more pertinent to judicial concerns. In particular, the value that French lawyers place on the pithy, analytical *note d'arrêt* which appears alongside the case report means that the legal academy is predominantly responsible for the production of a body of legal literature which judges generally read and respect."

Bibliography

Part I

Continental Legal History, A General Survey by Various European Authors, Association of American Law Schools, Little Brown and Company, 1912.

Dawson, John P., *The Oracles of the Law*, Ann Harbor: University of Michigan School of Law, 1968.

Esmein, A., *Précis Elémentaire de l'Histoire du Droit Français, de 1789 à 1814: Révolution, Consulat & Empire*, Paris: Librairie de la Société du Recueil Sirey, 1911.

Fresquet, R. de., *Traité Elémentaire de Droit Romain*, Paris: A. Marescq et Dujardin, Etienne Giraud, 1854.

Head, John W., *Great Legal Traditions: Civil Law, Common Law, and Chinese Law in Historical and Operational Perspective*, Carolina Academic Press, 2011.

Langbein, John H. et al., *History of the Common Law: The Development of Anglo-American Legal Institutions*, Aspen Publishers, Wolters Kluwer, 2009.

Le Code civil, 1804–1904: livre du centenaire, Paris: Arthur Rousseau, 1904.

Lesaffer, Randall, *European Legal History: A Cultural and Political Perspective*, 1st ed., Cambridge University Press, 2009.

Levasseur, Alain and Vicenç FELIÚ, *Moreau Lislet: The Man behind the Digest of 1808*, Claitor's Publishing Division, Baton Rouge, 2008.

Plucknett, Theodore F.T., *A Concise History of the Common Law*, 5th ed. Little Brown and Company, 1956.

Robinson, O.F. et al., *European Legal History*, 2nd ed., Butterworths, 1994.

Seagle, William, *The History of Law*, New York: Tudor Publishing Co., 1946.

Stein, Peter, *Roman Law in European History*, Cambridge University Press, 1999.

Versteeg, Russ, *The Essentials of Greek and Roman Law*, Carolina Academic Press, 2010.

Watkin, Thomas Glyn, *An Historical Introduction to Modern Civil Law*, Dartmouth: Ashgate, 1999.

Watson, Alan, *The Making of the Civil Law*, Harvard University Press, 1981.

Part II

Bergel, Jean-Louis, *Méthodologie juridique*, Presses Universitaires de France, 2001.

Bergel, Jean-Louis, *Théorie Générale du Droit*, 5è éd. Dalloz, 2012.

Cornu, Gérard, *Droit Civil: Introduction au droit*, 13è éd, collection Domat droit prive, Montchrestien, 2007.

Cornu, Gérard, *Linguistique juridique*, 3ème éd., collection Domat droit prive, Montchrestien, 2005.

Côté, Pierre-André, *The Interpretation of Legislation in Canada*, 4th ed., Carswell, Thomson Reuters Canada Ltd., 2011.

Dictionary of the Civil Code; Gérard Cornu, Association Henri Capitant; translation Alain Levasseur and Marie-Eugénie Laporte-Legeais; scientific coordination Juriscope; LexisNexis 2014.

Fabreguettes, M. P., *La Logique Judiciaire et l'Art de Juger*, 2è éd., L G D J, 1926.

French Civil Code, as of 1st July 2013, Legifrance; translation by D.Gruning (Loyola School of Law, New Orleans); Revision: Juriscope; Expert Committee: Alain Levasseur and John R. Trahan (Louisiana State University, Law Center, Baton Rouge).

Gémar, Jean-Claude and Nicholas KASIRER, *Jurilinguistique: entre langues et droits*; Jurilinguistics: Between Law and Language, Montréal, Thémis/Bruylant, 2005.

Le droit civil, avant tout un Style?, sous la direction de Nicholas KASIRER, les Editions Thémis, 2003.

Louisiana Civil Code, edited by Alain Levasseur, LexisNexis Civil Code Series, 2015.

Perelman, C., *Méthodes du Droit, Logique Juridique-Nouvelle rhétorique*, Dalloz, 1976.

Portalis, Jean-Etienne-Marie, *Ecrits et Discours Juridiques et Politiques*, Presses Universitaires d'Aix-Marseille, 1988.

Scalia, Antonin and Amy Gutmann, editor, "A Matter of Interpretation:
    . Federal Courts and the Law," Princeton University Press, 1997.
Singer, Norman J., *Statutes and Statutory Construction*, 4th ed., Callaghan,
    1984.

Index